T0046412

2ND EDITION

Birds *of* California

Field Guide

Stan Tekiela

Adventure Publications
Cambridge, Minnesota

Edited by Sandy Livoti and Dan Downing

Cover, book design and illustrations by Jonathan Norberg

Range maps produced by Anthony Hertzel

Proofreader: Emily Beaumont

10 9 8 7 6 5 4 3 2
Birds of California Field Guide
First Edition 2003
Second Edition 2022
Copyright © 2003 and 2022 by Stan Tekiela
Published by Adventure Publications
An imprint of AdventureKEEN
310 Garfield Street South
Cambridge, Minnesota 55008
(800) 678-7006
www.adventurepublications.net
Printed in China
ISBN 978-1-64755-198-8 (pbk.); ISBN 978-1-64755-199-5 (ebook)

TABLE OF CONTENTS

WHAT'S NEW?

It is hard to believe that it's been more than 15 years since the debut of *Birds of California Field Guide*. This critically acclaimed field guide has helped countless people identify and enjoy the birds that we love. Now, in this expanded second edition, *Birds of California Field Guide* introduces many new and exciting changes and a fresh look, while retaining the same familiar, easy-to-use format.

To help you identify even more birds in California, I have added 7 new species and more than 150 new color photographs. All of the range maps have been meticulously reviewed, and many updates have been made to reflect the ever-changing movements of the birds.

Everyone's favorite section, "Stan's Notes," has been expanded to include even more natural history information. "Compare" sections have been updated to help ensure that you correctly identify your bird, and additional feeder information has been added to help with bird feeding. I hope you will enjoy this great new edition as you continue to learn about and appreciate our California birds!

WHY WATCH BIRDS IN CALIFORNIA?

Millions of people have discovered bird feeding. It's a simple and enjoyable way to bring the beauty of birds closer to your home. Watching birds at your feeder often leads to a lifetime pursuit of bird identification. The *Birds of California Field Guide* is for those who want to identify the common birds of California.

There are over 1,100 bird species in North America. In California alone there have been over 510 different kinds of birds recorded throughout the years. These bird sightings have been documented by hundreds of bird watchers and have become a part of the official state record. From these valuable records, I've chosen 177 of the most common birds of California to include in this field guide.

Bird watching, or birding, is one of the most popular activities in America. Its appeal in California is due, in part, to an unusually rich and abundant birdlife. Why are there so many birds? One reason is open space. California is the third largest state, with more than 163,000 square miles (422,168 sq. km) and about 39.5 million people. On average, that is only 242 people per square mile (93 per sq. km). Most are located in southern California.

Open space is not the only reason there is such an abundance of birds. It's also the diversity of habitat. California can be broken into four distinctive habitats—the Pacific Border Province, Sierra-Cascade Province, Basin and Range Province and Lower California Province—each of which supports different groups of birds.

The Pacific Border Province, or Coastal Uplands, extends nearly the entire length of the coast along western California. Many of California's residents live here. This mainly mountainous region has many ridges, large valleys and several ranges, with elevations reaching 9,000 feet (2,750 m). This is a good place to see birds such as the California Towhee.

The Sierra-Cascade Province is a vast region that extends from Oregon to southern California. Located east of the Pacific Border, it is a belt of rugged mountain ranges with high peaks and deep valleys. Mount Whitney, the highest peak in the U.S. outside of Alaska, is in this province. This region is heavily forested and is a good place to see Clark's Nutcrackers and Steller's Jays.

To the east of the Sierra-Cascade Province is the Basin and Range Province. Most of this region is flat, dry and sparsely vegetated, with low elevation deserts such as Death Valley and the Sonoran Desert. Usually receiving less than 2 inches (5 cm) of rainfall per year, this province is home to many wonderful birds such as Black-throated Sparrows and various hummingbird species.

The Lower California Province is the designation most of the southern part of the state. With its rolling mountains and valleys, it's a good place to see the California Gnatcatcher, a species of special concern.

Water also plays a big part in California's bird populations. There are 840 miles (1,352 km) of coastline, with a total of 3,427 miles (5,517 km) of coast, including all the inlets and islands. The coast is a great place to see many gull species such as California Gull or Heermann's Gull. California also has over 2,675 square miles (6,950 sq. km) of fresh water surface. The Sacramento and San Joaquin Rivers are the largest, and several drain the entire state. There are also several thousand small lakes. Salton Sea and Lake Tahoe are the largest and are home to birds such as American Avocets and American White Pelicans. It's always worth the time to investigate bodies of water in California for the presence of birds.

Varying habitats in California also mean variations in weather. California has the highest and lowest elevations in the lower

48 states, rising from 282 feet (86 m) below sea level in Death Valley to 14,494 feet (4,419 m) at Mount Whitney. Northern parts of California are cooler and moister than southern California. The Mojave Desert is the hottest region in California and the U.S. in the summer, while winters in the mountains are cold and snowy with many snowcapped peaks year-round.

No matter if you're in the hot, arid deserts or in the cool, moist mountains of California, there are birds to watch in each season. Whether witnessing hawks migrating in autumn or welcoming back hummingbirds in spring, there is variety and excitement in birding in the Golden State.

OBSERVE WITH A STRATEGY: TIPS FOR IDENTIFYING BIRDS

Identifying birds isn't as difficult as you might think. By simply following a few basic strategies, you can increase your chances of successfully identifying most birds that you see. One of the first and easiest things to do when you see a new bird is to note **its color.** This field guide is organized by color, so simply turn to the right color section to find it.

Next, note the **size of the bird.** A strategy to quickly estimate size is to compare different birds. Pick a small, a medium and a large bird. Select an American Robin as the medium bird. Measured from bill tip to tail tip, a robin is 10 inches (25 cm). Now select two other birds, one smaller and one larger. Good choices are a House Sparrow, at about 6 inches (15 cm), and an American Crow, around 18 inches (45 cm). When you see a species you don't know, you can now quickly ask yourself, "Is it larger than a sparrow but smaller than a robin?" When you look in your field guide to identify your bird, check the species that are roughly 6–10 inches (15–25 cm). This will help to narrow your choices.

Next, note the **size, shape and color of the bill.** Is it long or short, thick or thin, pointed or blunt, curved or straight? Seed-eating birds, such as Blue Grosbeaks, have bills that are thick and strong enough to crack even the toughest seeds. Birds that sip nectar, such as Black-chinned Hummingbirds, need long, thin bills to reach deep into flowers. Hawks and owls tear their prey with very sharp, curving bills. Sometimes, just noting the bill shape can help you decide whether the bird is a woodpecker, finch, grosbeak, blackbird or bird of prey.

Next, take a look around and note the **habitat** in which you see the bird. Is it wading in a saltwater marsh? Walking along a riverbank or on the beach? Soaring in the sky? Is it perched high in the trees or hopping along the forest floor? Because of diet and habitat preferences, you'll often see robins hopping on the ground but not usually eating seeds at a feeder. Or you'll see a Black-headed Grosbeak sitting on a tree branch but not climbing headfirst down the trunk, like a Red-breasted Nuthatch would.

Noticing **what the bird is eating** will give you another clue to help you identify the species. Feeding is a big part of any bird's life. Fully one-third of all bird activity revolves around searching for food, catching prey and eating. While birds don't always follow all the rules of their diet, you can make some general assumptions. Northern Flickers, for instance, feed on ants and other insects, so you wouldn't expect to see them visiting a seed feeder. Other birds, such as Barn and Cliff Swallows, eat flying insects and spend hours swooping and diving to catch a meal.

Sometimes you can identify a bird by **the way it perches.** Body posture can help you differentiate between an American Crow and a Red-tailed Hawk, for example. Crows lean forward over their feet on a branch, while hawks perch in a vertical position.

Consider posture the next time you see an unidentified large bird in a tree.

Birds in flight are harder to identify, but noting the **wing size and shape** will help. Wing size is in direct proportion to body size, weight and type of flight. Wing shape determines whether the bird flies fast and with precision, or slowly and less precisely. Barn Swallows, for instance, have short, pointed wings that slice through the air, enabling swift, accurate flight. Turkey Vultures have long, broad wings for soaring on warm updrafts. House Finches have short, rounded wings, helping them to flit through thick tangles of branches.

Some bird species have a unique **pattern of flight** that can help in identification. American Goldfinches fly in a distinctive undulating pattern that makes it look like they're riding a roller coaster.

While it's not easy to make all of these observations in the short time you often have to watch a "mystery" bird, practicing these identification methods will greatly expand your birding skills. To further improve your skills, seek the guidance of a more experienced birder who can answer your questions on the spot.

BIRD BASICS

It's easier to identify birds and communicate about them if you know the names of the different parts of a bird. For instance, it's more effective to use the word "crest" to indicate the set of extra-long feathers on top of the head of a Steller's Jay than to try to describe it.

The following illustration points out the basic parts of a bird. Because it is a composite of many birds, it shouldn't be confused with any actual bird.

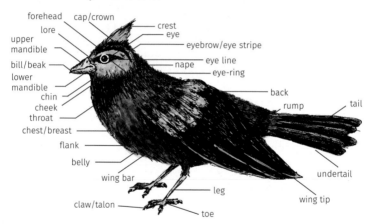

Bird Color Variables

No other animal has a color palette like a bird's. Brilliant blues, lemon yellows, showy reds and iridescent greens are common in the bird world. In general, male birds are more colorful than their female counterparts. This helps the male attract a mate, essentially saying, "Hey, look at me!" Color calls attention to a male's health as well. The better the condition of his feathers, the better his food source, territory and potential for mating.

Male and female birds that don't look like each other are called sexually dimorphic, meaning "two forms." Dimorphic females often have a nondescript dull color, as seen in Lazuli Buntings. Muted tones help females hide during the weeks of motionless incubation and draw less attention to them when they're out feeding or taking a break from the rigors of raising the young.

The males of some species, such as the Hairy Woodpecker, Steller's Jay and Bald Eagle, look nearly identical to the females. In woodpeckers, the sexes are differentiated by only a red mark, or sometimes a yellow mark. Depending on the species, the mark may be on top of the head, on the face or nape of the neck, or just behind the bill.

During the first year, juvenile birds often look like their mothers. Since brightly colored feathers are used mainly for attracting a mate, young non-breeding males don't have a need for colorful plumage. It's not until the first spring molt (or several years later, depending on the species) that young males obtain their breeding colors.

Both breeding and winter plumages are the result of molting. Molting is the process of dropping old, worn feathers and replacing them with new ones. All birds molt, typically twice a year, with the spring molt usually occurring in late winter. At this time, most birds produce their brighter breeding plumage, which lasts throughout the summer.

Winter plumage is the result of the late summer molt, which serves a couple of important functions. First, it adds feathers for warmth in the coming winter season. Second, in some species it produces feathers that tend to be drab in color, which helps to camouflage the birds and hide them from predators. The winter plumage of the male American Goldfinch, for example, is olive-brown, unlike its canary-yellow breeding color during summer. Luckily for us, some birds, such as the male Lewis's Woodpeckers, retain their bright summer colors all year long.

Bird Nests

Bird nests are a true feat of engineering. Imagine constructing a home that's strong enough to weather storms, large enough to hold your entire family, insulated enough to shelter them from cold and heat, and waterproof enough to keep out rain. Think about building it without blueprints or directions and using mainly your feet. Birds do this!

Before building, birds must select an appropriate site. In some species, such as the House Wren, the male picks out several potential sites and assembles small twigs in each. The "extra" nests, called dummy nests, discourage other birds from using any nearby cavities for their nests. The male takes the female around and shows her the choices. After choosing her favorite, she finishes the construction.

In other species, such as the Bullock's Oriole, the female selects the site and builds the nest, while the male offers an occasional suggestion. Each bird species has its own nest-building routine that is strictly followed.

As you can see in these illustrations, birds build a wide variety of nest types.

| ground nest | platform nest | cup nest | pendulous nest | cavity nest |

Nesting material often consists of natural items found in the immediate area. Most nests consist of plant fibers (such as bark from grapevines), sticks, mud, dried grass, feathers, fur, or soft, fuzzy tufts from thistle. Some birds, including Black-chinned Hummingbirds, use spiderwebs to glue nest materials together.

Transportation of nesting material is limited to the amount a bird can hold or carry. Birds must make many trips afield to gather enough material to complete a nest. Most nests take four days or more—and hundreds, if not thousands, of trips—to build.

A **ground nest** can be a mound of vegetation on the ground or in the water. It can also be just a simple, shallow depression scraped out in earth, stones or sand. Killdeer and Horned Larks scrape out ground nests without adding any nesting material.

The **platform nest** represents a much more complex type of construction. Typically built with twigs or sticks and branches, this nest forms a platform and has a depression in the center to nestle the eggs. Platform nests can be in trees; on balconies, cliffs, bridges, or man-made platforms; and even in flowerpots. They often provide space for the adventurous young and function as a landing platform for the parents.

Mourning Doves and herons don't anchor their platform nests to trees, so these can tumble from branches during high winds and storms. Hawks, eagles, ospreys and other birds construct sturdier platform nests with large sticks and branches.

Other platform nests are constructed on the ground with mud, grass and other vegetation from the area. Many waterfowl build platform nests on the ground near or in water. A **floating platform nest** moves with the water level, preventing the nest, eggs and birds from being flooded.

Three-quarters of all songbirds construct a **cup nest,** which is a modified platform nest. The supporting platform is built first and attached firmly to a tree, shrub, or rock ledge or the ground. Next, the sides are constructed with grass, small twigs, bark or leaves, which are woven together and often glued with mud for added strength. The inner cup can be lined with down feathers, animal fur or hair, or soft plant materials and is contoured last.

The **pendulous nest** is an unusual nest that looks like a sock hanging from a branch. Attached to the end of small branches of trees, this unique nest is inaccessible to most predators and often waves wildly in a breeze.

Woven tightly with plant fibers, the pendulous nest is strong and watertight and takes up to a week to build. A small opening at the top or on the side allows parents access to the grass-lined interior. More commonly used by tropical birds, this complex nest has also been mastered by orioles and kinglets. It must be one heck of a ride to be inside one of these nests during a windy spring thunderstorm!

The **cavity nest** is used by many species of birds, most notably woodpeckers and Western Bluebirds. A cavity nest is often excavated from a branch or tree trunk and offers shelter from storms, sun, cold and predators. A small entrance hole in a tree can lead to a nest chamber that is up to a safe 10 inches (25 cm) deep.

Typically made by woodpeckers, cavity nests are usually used only once by the builder. Nest cavities can be used for many subsequent years by birds such as bluebirds, which do not have the capability to excavate their own. Kingfishers, on the other hand, can dig a tunnel up to 4 feet (about 1 m) long in a riverbank. The nest chamber at the end of the tunnel is already well insulated, so it's usually only sparsely lined.

One of the most clever of all nests is the **no nest,** or daycare nest. Parasitic birds, such as cowbirds, don't build their own nests. Instead, the egg-laden female searches out the nest of another bird and sneaks in to lay an egg while the host mother isn't looking.

A mother cowbird wastes no energy building a nest only to have it raided by a predator. Laying her eggs in the nests of other birds transfers the responsibility of raising her young to the host. When she lays her eggs in several nests, the chances increase that at least one of her babies will live to maturity.

Who Builds the Nest?

Generally, the female bird constructs the nest. She gathers the materials and does the building, with an occasional visit from her mate to check on progress. In some species, both parents contribute equally to nest building. The male may forage for sticks, grass or mud, but it is the female that often fashions the nest. Only rarely does a male build a nest by himself.

Fledging

Fledging is the time between hatching and flight, or leaving the nest. Some species of birds are **precocial,** meaning they leave the nest within hours of hatching, though it may be weeks before they can fly. This is common in waterfowl and shorebirds.

Baby birds that hatch naked and blind need to stay in the nest for a few weeks (these birds are **altricial**). Baby birds that are still in the nest are **nestlings.** Until birds start to fly, they are called **fledglings.**

Why Birds Migrate

Why do so many species of birds migrate? The short answer is simple: food. Birds migrate to locations with abundant food, as it is easier to breed where there is food than where food is scarce. Western Tanagers, for instance, are **complete migrators** that fly from the tropics of Central America and Mexico to nest in the forests of North America, where billions of newly hatched insects are available as food for their young.

Other migrators, such as some birds of prey, travel back to northern regions in spring. In these locations, they hunt mice, voles and other small rodents that are beginning to breed.

Complete migrators have a set time and pattern of migration. Every year at nearly the same time, they head to a specific wintering ground. Complete migrators may travel great distances, sometimes 15,000 miles (24,100 km) or more in one year.

Complete migration doesn't necessarily imply flying from the cold, frozen northland to a tropical destination. The Black-chinned Hummingbird, for example, is a complete migrator that flies from California to Central and South America. This trip is still considered complete migration.

Complete migrators have many interesting aspects. In spring, males often leave a few weeks before the females, arriving early to scope out possibilities for nesting sites and food sources, and to begin to defend territories. The females arrive several weeks later. In many species, the females and their young leave earlier in the fall, often up to four weeks before the adult males.

Other species, such as the Lesser Goldfinch, are **partial migrators.** These birds usually wait until their food supplies dwindle before flying south. Unlike complete migrators, partial migrators move only far enough south, or sometimes east and west, to find abundant food. In some years it might be only a few hundred miles, while in other years it can be as much as 1,000. This kind of migration, dependent on weather and the availability of food, is sometimes called seasonal movement.

Unlike the predictable complete migrators or partial migrators, **irruptive migrators** can move every third to fifth year or, in some cases, in consecutive years. These migrations are triggered when times are tough and food is scarce. Red-breasted Nuthatches are irruptive migrators. They leave their normal northern range in search of more food or in response to overpopulation.

Many other birds don't migrate at all. Mountain Chickadees, for example, are **non-migrators** that remain in their habitat all year long and just move around as necessary to find food.

How Do Birds Migrate?

One of the many secrets of migration is fat. While most people are fighting the ongoing battle of the bulge, birds intentionally gorge themselves to gain as much fat as possible without losing the ability to fly. Fat provides the greatest amount of energy per unit of weight. In the same way that your car needs gas, birds are propelled by fat and stall without it.

During long migratory flights, fat deposits are used up quickly, and birds need to stop to refuel. This is when backyard bird feeding stations and undeveloped, natural spaces around our towns and cities are especially important. Some birds require up to 2–3 days of constant feeding to build their fat reserves before continuing their seasonal trip.

Many birds, such as most eagles, hawks, ospreys, falcons and vultures, migrate during the day. Larger birds can hold more body fat, go longer without eating and take longer to migrate. These birds glide along on rising columns of warm air, called thermals, that hold them aloft while they slowly make their way north or south. They generally rest at night and hunt early in the morning before the sun has a chance to warm the land and create good soaring conditions. Daytime migrators use a combination of landforms, rivers, and the rising and setting sun to guide them in the right direction.

The majority of small birds, called **passerines,** migrate at night. Studies show that some use the stars to navigate. Others use the setting sun, and still others, such as pigeons, use Earth's magnetic field to guide them north or south.

While flying at night may not seem like a good idea, it's actually safer. First, there are fewer avian predators hunting for birds at night. Second, night travel allows time during the day to find food in unfamiliar surroundings. Third, wind patterns at night tend to be flat, or laminar. Flat winds don't have the turbulence of daytime winds and can help push the smaller birds along.

HOW TO USE THIS GUIDE

To help you quickly and easily identify birds, this field guide is organized by color. Refer to the color key on the first page, note the color of the bird, and turn to that section. For example, the Williamson's Sapsucker is black and white with a yellow belly. Because the bird is mostly black and white, it will be found in the black-and-white section.

Each color section is also arranged by size, generally with the smaller birds first. Sections may also incorporate the average size in a range, which in some cases reflects size differences between male and female birds. Flip through the pages in the color section to find the bird. If you already know the name of the bird, check the index for the page number.

In some species, the male and female are very different in color. In others, the breeding and winter plumage colors differ. These species will have an inset photograph with a page reference and will be found in two color sections.

You will find a variety of information in the bird description sections. To learn more, turn to the sample on pp. 22–23.

Range Maps

Range maps are included for each bird. Colored areas indicate where the bird is frequently found. The colors represent the presence of a species during a specific season, not the density, or amount, of birds in the area. Green is used for summer, blue for winter, red for year-round and yellow for migration.

While every effort has been made to depict accurate ranges, these are constantly in flux due to a variety of factors. Changing weather, habitat, species abundance and availability of vital resources, such as food and water, can affect the migration and movement of local populations, causing birds to be found in areas that are atypical for the species. So please use the maps as intended—as general guides only.

female
p. 163

male

Common Name

Scientific name Color Indicator —

YEAR-ROUND
SUMMER
MIGRATION
WINTER

Size:	measurement is from head to tip of tail; wingspan may be listed as well
Male:	brief description of the male bird; may include breeding, winter or other plumages
Female:	brief description of the female bird, which is sometimes different from the male
Juvenile:	brief description of the juvenile bird, which often looks like the adult female
Nest:	kind of nest the bird builds to raise its young; who builds it; number of broods per year
Eggs:	number of eggs you might expect to see in a nest; color and marking
Incubation:	average days the parents spend incubating the eggs; who does the incubation
Fledging:	average days the young spend in the nest after hatching but before they leave the nest; who does the most "childcare" and feeding
Migration:	type of migrator: complete (seasonal, consistent), partial (seasonal, destination varies), irruptive (unpredictable, depends on the food supply) or non-migrator
Food:	what the bird eats most of the time (e.g., seeds, insects, fruit, nectar, small mammals, fish) and whether it typically comes to a bird feeder
Compare:	notes about other birds that look similar and the pages on which they can be found; may include extra information to aid in identification

Stan's Notes: Interesting natural history information. This could be something to look or listen for or something to help positively identify the bird. Also includes remarkable features.

female
p. 169

male

Brown-headed Cowbird
Molothrus ater

YEAR-ROUND
SUMMER

Size: 7½" (19 cm)

Male: Glossy black with a chocolate-brown head. Dark eyes. Pointed, sharp gray bill.

Female: dull brown with a pointed, sharp, gray bill

Juvenile: similar to female but with dull-gray plumage and a streaked chest

Nest: no nest; lays eggs in nests of other birds

Eggs: 5–7; white with brown markings

Incubation: 10–13 days; host birds incubate eggs

Fledging: 10–11 days; host birds feed the young

Migration: non-migrator to partial in California

Food: insects, seeds; will come to seed feeders

Compare: The male Red-winged Blackbird (p. 33) is slightly larger with red-and-yellow patches on upper wings. European Starling (p. 27) has a shorter tail.

Stan's Notes: Cowbirds are members of the blackbird family. Of approximately 750 species of parasitic birds worldwide, this is the only parasitic bird in the state. Brood parasites lay their eggs in the nests of other birds, leaving the host birds to raise their young. Cowbirds are known to have laid their eggs in the nests of over 200 species of birds. While some birds reject cowbird eggs, most incubate them and raise the young, even to the exclusion of their own. Look for warblers and other birds feeding young birds twice their own size. Named "cowbird" for its habit of following bison and cattle herds to feed on insects flushed up by the animals.

winter

breeding

European Starling
Sturnus vulgaris

YEAR-ROUND

Size: 7½" (19 cm)

Male: Glittering, iridescent purplish black in spring and summer; duller and speckled with white in fall and winter. Long, pointed, yellow bill in spring; gray in fall. Pointed wings. Short tail.

Female: same as male

Juvenile: similar to adults, with grayish-brown plumage and a streaked chest

Nest: cavity; male and female line cavity; 2 broods per year

Eggs: 4–6; bluish with brown markings

Incubation: 12–14 days; female and male incubate

Fledging: 18–20 days; female and male feed the young

Migration: non-migrator; moves around in winter to find food

Food: insects, seeds, fruit; visits seed or suet feeders

Compare: The male Brown-headed Cowbird (p. 25) has a brown head. Look for the shiny, dark feathers to help identify the European Starling.

Stan's Notes: A great songster, this bird can also mimic the songs of up to 20 bird species and imitate sounds, including the human voice. Jaws are more powerful when opening than when closing, enabling the bird to pry open crevices to find insects. Often displaces woodpeckers, chickadees and other cavity-nesting birds. Large families gather with blackbirds in the fall. Not a native bird; 100 starlings were introduced to New York City in 1890–91 from Europe. Bill changes color in spring and fall.

female
p. 309

male

Phainopepla
Phainopepla nitens

YEAR-ROUND
SUMMER

Size: 8" (20 cm)

Male: Slim, long, glossy black bird with a ragged crest and deep red eyes. Wing patches near tips of wings are white, obvious in flight.

Female: slim, long, mostly gray bird with a ragged crest and deep red eyes, whitish wing bars

Juvenile: similar to female

Nest: cup; female and male construct; 1–2 broods per year

Eggs: 2–4; gray with brown markings

Incubation: 12–14 days; female and male incubate

Fledging: 18–20 days; female and male feed young

Migration: partial migrator, to southern California and Arizona

Food: fruit (usually mistletoe), insects; will come to water elements or water drips in yards

Compare: The only all-black bird with a crest and red eyes. Look for white wing patches in flight.

Stan's Notes: Seen in desert scrub with water and mistletoe nearby. Gives a low, liquid "kweer" song, but will also mimic other species. In winter, individuals defend food supply, such as a single tree with abundant mistletoe berries. Probably responsible for the dispersal of mistletoe plants far and wide. Male will fly up to a height of 300 feet (90 m), circling and zigzagging to court female. Builds nest of twigs and plant fibers and binds it with spider webs in the crotch of a mistletoe cluster. Lines nest with hair or soft plant fibers. May be the only species to nest in two regions in the same nesting season. Nests in dry desert habitat in early spring, and when it gets hot, moves to a higher area with an abundant water supply to nest again.

Spotted Towhee

Pipilo maculatus

YEAR-ROUND WINTER

Size: 8½" (22 cm)

Male: Mostly black with dirty red-brown sides and a white belly. Multiple white spots on wings and sides. Long black tail with a white tip. Rich, red eyes.

Female: very similar to male but with a brown head

Juvenile: brown with a heavily streaked chest

Nest: cup; female builds; 1–2 broods per year

Eggs: 3–5; white with brown markings

Incubation: 12–14 days; female and male incubate

Fledging: 10–12 days; female and male feed young

Migration: non-migrator to partial migrator; moves around in winter to find food

Food: seeds, fruit, insects

Compare: Closely related to the Green-tailed Towhee (p. 365), which lacks the bold black and red colors. California Towhee (p. 187) is larger and lacks rusty-red sides.

Stan's Notes: Not as common as the Green-tailed Towhee, but it inhabits similar areas. Found in a variety of habitats, from thick brush and chaparral to suburban backyards. Usually heard noisily scratching through dead leaves on the ground for food. Over 70 percent of its diet is plant material. Eats more insects during spring and summer. Well known to retreat from danger by walking away rather than taking to flight. Nest is nearly always on the ground under bushes but away from where the male perches to sing. Begins breeding in April. Lays eggs in May. After the breeding season, moves to higher elevations. Song and plumage vary geographically and aren't well studied or understood.

female
p. 181

male

Red-winged Blackbird
Agelaius phoeniceus

YEAR-ROUND

Size:	8½" (22 cm)
Male:	Jet black with red-and-yellow patches (epaulets) on upper wings. Pointed black bill.
Female:	heavily streaked brown with a pointed brown bill and white eyebrows
Juvenile:	same as female
Nest:	cup; female builds; 2–3 broods per year
Eggs:	3–4; bluish green with brown markings
Incubation:	10–12 days; female incubates
Fledging:	11–14 days; female and male feed the young
Migration:	non-migrator to partial; will move around the state to find food in winter
Food:	seeds, insects; visits seed and suet feeders
Compare:	The male Tricolored Blackbird (p. 35) has red-and-white shoulder patches (epaulets). The male Brown-headed Cowbird (p. 25) is smaller and glossier and has a brown head. The bold red-and-yellow epaulets distinguish the male Red-winged from other blackbirds.

Stan's Notes: One of the most widespread and numerous birds in the state. Found around marshes, wetlands, lakes and rivers. Flocks with as many as 10,000 birds have been reported. Males arrive before the females and sing to defend their territory. The male repeats his call from the top of a cattail while showing off his red-and-yellow shoulder patches. The female chooses a mate and often builds her nest over shallow water in a thick stand of cattails. The male can be aggressive when defending the nest. Red-winged Blackbirds feed mostly on seeds in spring and fall, and insects throughout the summer.

female
p. 183

Tricolored Blackbird
Agelaius tricolor

YEAR-ROUND

Size:	9" (22.5 cm)
Male:	Black with red and white shoulder patches (epaulets). Pointed dark bill and very dark reddish brown eyes.
Female:	overall dark brown, gray chin and breast, pointed dark bill, black legs, dark reddish brown eyes
Juvenile:	similar to female, but not as brown
Nest:	cup; female builds; 2 broods per year
Eggs:	3–4; pale green with brown markings
Incubation:	11–13 days; female incubates
Fledging:	11–14 days; female and male feed young
Migration:	non-migrator to partial migrator; will move around to find food
Food:	insects, seeds, grain; visits ground feeders
Compare:	The male Red-winged Blackbird (p. 33) is similar, but has red and yellow epaulets.

Stan's Notes: Blackbird species found mainly in California. Very closely related to Red-winged Blackbirds. Tricolored usually has a smaller bill than Red-winged. Flocks with Red-wingeds and other blackbirds during winter, moving around to find food and nesting colonies. Sometimes moves from one area to another for unknown reasons. Tricoloreds and Red-wingeds have some of the highest nesting densities of any bird species, with some colonies in the tens of thousands. Like the Red-winged, it nests in shallow freshwater marshes. Builds nest from woven sedges, grasses and other green plants. Attaches nest to upright cattail stems and lines it with finer plant fibers. Young are fed mainly insects.

male

female
p. 185

Brewer's Blackbird
Euphagus cyanocephalus

YEAR-ROUND
SUMMER
WINTER

Size: 9" (22.5 cm)

Male: Overall glossy black, shining green in direct light. Head more purple than green. Bright-white or pale-yellow eyes. Winter plumage can be dull gray to black.

Female: similar to male, only overall grayish brown, most have dark eyes

Juvenile: similar to female

Nest: cup; female builds; 1–2 broods per year

Eggs: 4–6; gray with brown markings

Incubation: 12–14 days; female incubates

Fledging: 13–14 days; female and male feed young

Migration: non-migrator to partial in California; moves around to find food

Food: insects, seeds, fruit

Compare: Male Great-tailed Grackle (p. 47) is larger and has a very long tail. The male Brown-headed Cowbird (p. 25) is smaller and has a brown head. Male Red-winged Blackbird (p. 33) has red-and-yellow shoulder marks.

Stan's Notes: Common blackbird often found in association with agricultural lands and seen in open areas such as wet pastures, and mountain meadows up to 10,000 feet (3,050 m). Male and some females are easily identified by their bright, nearly white eyes. It is a common cowbird host, usually nesting in a shrub, small tree or directly on the ground. Prefers to nest in small colonies of up to 20 pairs. Gathers in large flocks with cowbirds, Red-wingeds and other blackbirds to migrate. It is expanding its range in North America.

male

Yellow-headed Blackbird
Xanthocephalus xanthocephalus

YEAR-ROUND
SUMMER
MIGRATION
WINTER

Size: 9–11" (23–28 cm)

Male: Large black bird with a lemon-yellow head, breast and nape of neck. Black mask and gray bill. White wing patches.

Female: similar to male but slightly smaller with a brown body and dull-yellow head and chest

Juvenile: similar to female

Nest: cup; female builds; 2 broods per year

Eggs: 3–5; greenish white with brown markings

Incubation: 11–13 days; female incubates

Fledging: 9–12 days; female feeds the young

Migration: complete, to parts of California, Mexico

Food: insects, seeds; will come to ground feeders

Compare: The male Red-winged Blackbird (p. 33) is smaller and has red-and-yellow patches on its wings. Look for the bright-yellow head to identify the male Yellow-headed.

Stan's Notes: Found around marshes, wetlands and lakes. Nests in deep water, unlike its cousin, the Red-winged Blackbird, which prefers shallow water. Usually heard before seen. Gives a raspy, low, metallic-sounding call. The male is the only large black bird with a bright-yellow head. He gives an impressive mating display, flying with his head drooped and feet and tail pointing down while steadily beating his wings. Young keep low and out of sight for up to three weeks before they start to fly. Migrates in large flocks of as many as 200 birds, often with Red-winged Blackbirds and Brown-headed Cowbirds. Flocks of mainly males return in early April; females return later. Most colonies consist of 20–100 nests.

Common Gallinule
Gallinula galeata

Size: 13–15" (33–38 cm)

Male: Nearly black overall with yellow-tipped red bill. Red forehead. Thin line of white along sides. Yellowish-green legs.

Female: same as male

Juvenile: same as adult, but brown with white throat and dirty-yellow legs

Nest: ground; female and male build; 1–2 broods per year

Eggs: 2–10; brown with dark markings

Incubation: 19–22 days; female and male incubate

Fledging: 40–50 days; female and male feed the young

Migration: non-migrator to partial in California

Food: insects, snails, seeds, green leaves, fruit

Compare: American Coot (p. 43) is similar in size but lacks the distinctive yellow-tipped bill and red forehead of Common Gallinule.

Stan's Notes: Also known as Mud Hen or Pond Chicken. A nearly all-black duck-like bird often seen in freshwater marshes and lakes. Walks on floating vegetation or swims while hunting for insects. Females known to lay eggs in other gallinule nests in addition to their own. Builds its nest with cattails and bulrushes and sometimes takes an old nest in a low shrub. A cooperative breeder, having young of first brood help raise young of second. Young leave nest usually within a few hours after hatching but stay with the family for a couple of months. Young ride on backs of adults.

American Coot
Fulica americana

YEAR-ROUND

Size: 13–16" (33–40 cm)

Male: Gray-to-black waterbird. Duck-like white bill with a dark band near the tip and a small red patch near the eyes. Small white patch near base of tail. Green legs and feet. Red eyes.

Female: same as male

Juvenile: much paler than adults, with a gray bill

Nest: floating platform; female and male construct; 1 brood per year

Eggs: 9–12; pinkish buff with brown markings

Incubation: 21–25 days; female and male incubate

Fledging: 49–52 days; female and male feed young

Migration: non-migrator in California

Food: insects, aquatic plants

Compare: Smaller than most waterfowl, it is the only black, duck-like bird with a white bill.

Stan's Notes: Usually seen in large flocks on open water. Not a duck, as it has large lobed toes instead of webbed feet. An excellent diver and swimmer, bobbing its head as it swims. A favorite food of Bald Eagles. It is not often seen in flight, unless it's trying to escape from an eagle. To take off, it scrambles across the surface of the water, flapping its wings. Gives a unique series of creaks, groans and clicks. Anchors its floating platform nest to vegetation. Huge flocks with as many as 1,000 birds gather for migration. Migrates at night. The common name "coot" comes from the Middle English word *coote*, which was used to describe various waterfowl. Like the Common Gallinule, the American Coot is also called Mud Hen.

Black Oystercatcher
Haematopus bachmani

Size: 18" (45 cm)

Male: An overall black body with a bright reddish orange, heavy straight bill. Yellow eyes with a red outline. Yellow legs and feet. Stocky body with a short tail and broad wings, as seen in flight.

Female: same as male

Juvenile: similar to adult, with light brown body and dull orange, black-tipped bill

Nest: ground; female and male construct; 1 brood per year

Eggs: 1–3; dull white to olive with brown marks

Incubation: 24–29 days; female incubates

Fledging: 35–40 days; female and male feed young

Migration: non-migrator to partial in California

Food: insects, mollusks, worms, crustaceans

Compare: American Avocet (p. 87) has longer legs and a black-and-white body. The breeding Black-bellied Plover (p. 73) has white on the head and a black-and-white back. Look for the stocky body and red-orange bill of Oystercatcher.

Stan's Notes: A shorebird found mainly along rocky shores. Rarely seen away from the coast. Often alone and not approachable. Common name comes from its ability to feed on oysters and mussels. Uses its large bill to pry or sometimes chisel shells open with hammer-like blows. Believed to have a long-term pair bond. A noisy courtship display with much mutual bowing. Nest is a scrape on the ground, sometimes lined with shells and rocks, built above the high tide.

female
p. 215

male

Great-tailed Grackle
Quiscalus mexicanus

Size: 18" (45 cm), male
15" (38 cm), female

Male: Large all-black bird with iridescent purple sheen on the head and back. Exceptionally long tail. Bright-yellow eyes.

Female: considerably smaller than the male, overall brown bird with gray-to-brown belly, light-brown-to-white eyes, eyebrows, throat and upper chest

Juvenile: similar to female

Nest: cup; female builds; 1–2 broods per year

Eggs: 3–5; greenish blue with brown markings

Incubation: 12–14 days; female incubates

Fledging: 21–23 days; female feeds young

Migration: non-migrator to partial migrator in California; moves around to find food

Food: insects, fruit, seeds; comes to seed feeders

Compare: Male Brown-headed Cowbird (p. 25) lacks the long tail and has a brown head.

Stan's Notes: This is our largest grackle. It was once considered a subspecies of the Boat-tailed Grackle, which occurs in Florida and along the East and Gulf Coasts. This bird prefers to nest near water in an open habitat. A colony nester. Males do not participate in nest building, incubation or raising young. Males rarely fight; females squabble over nest sites and materials. Several females mate with one male. They are expanding northward, moving into northern states. Western populations tend to be larger than the eastern. Song varies from population to population.

in flight

American Crow
Corvus brachyrhynchos

YEAR-ROUND WINTER

Size: 18" (45 cm)

Male: All-black bird with black bill, legs and feet. Can have a purple sheen in direct sunlight.

Female: same as male

Juvenile: same as adult

Nest: platform; female builds; 1 brood per year

Eggs: 4–6; bluish to olive-green with brown marks

Incubation: 18 days; female incubates

Fledging: 28–35 days; female and male feed the young

Migration: non-migrator to partial migrator; moves around to find food

Food: fruit, insects, mammals, fish, carrion; will come to seed and suet feeders

Compare: Common Raven (p. 51) is similar, but it has a larger bill and has shaggy throat feathers. Crow's call is higher than the raspy, low calls of ravens. Crow has a squared tail. Ravens have a wedge-shaped tail, apparent in flight. Black-billed Magpie (p. 91) has a long tail and white belly.

Stan's Notes: One of the most recognizable birds in the state. More common than its cousins, the ravens. Imitates other birds and human voices. One of the smartest of all birds and very social, often entertaining itself by provoking chases with other birds. Eats roadkill but is rarely hit by vehicles. Can live as long as 20 years. Often reuses its nest every year if it's not taken over by a Great Horned Owl. Unmated birds, known as helpers, help to raise the young. Extended families roost together at night, dispersing daily to hunt. Cannot soar on thermals; flaps constantly and glides downward.

in flight

Common Raven
Corvus corax

YEAR-ROUND

Size: 22–27" (56–69 cm)

Male: Large all-black bird with a shaggy beard of feathers on throat and chin. Large black bill. Large wedge-shaped tail, best seen in flight.

Female: same as male

Juvenile: same as adult

Nest: platform; female and male construct; 1 brood per year

Eggs: 4–6; pale green with brown markings

Incubation: 18–21 days; female incubates

Fledging: 38–44 days; female and male feed the young

Migration: non-migrator in California; will move around to find food

Food: insects, fruit, small animals, carrion

Compare: American Crow (p. 49) is smaller and lacks the shaggy throat feathers. Low raspy call, compared with the higher-pitched call of the American Crow. Glides on flat, outstretched wings, unlike the crow's slightly V-shaped wings.

Stan's Notes: Considered by some people to be the smartest of all birds. Known for its aerial acrobatics and long swooping dives. Soars on wind without flapping, like a raptor. Sometimes scavenges with crows and gulls. A cooperative hunter that often communicates the location of a good source of food to other ravens. Most start to breed at 3–4 years. Complex courtship includes grabbing bills, preening each other and cooing. Long-term pair bond. Uses the same nest site for many years.

soaring

juvenile

drying

Turkey Vulture
Cathartes aura

YEAR-ROUND
SUMMER

Size: 26–32" (66–80 cm); up to 6' wingspan

Male: Large and black with a naked red head and legs. In flight, wings are two-toned with a black leading edge and a gray trailing edge. Wing tips end in finger-like projections. Tail is long and squared. Ivory bill.

Female: same as male but slightly smaller

Juvenile: similar to adults, with a gray-to-blackish head and bill

Nest: no nest or minimal nest, on a cliff or in a cave, sometimes in a hollow tree; 1 brood per year

Eggs: 1–3; white with brown markings

Incubation: 38–41 days; female and male incubate

Fledging: 66–88 days; female and male feed the young

Migration: partial to non-migrator in California

Food: carrion; parents regurgitate to feed the young

Compare: California Condor (p. 101) is much larger with white wing linings. Bald Eagle (p. 99) is larger and lacks two-toned wings. Look for the obvious naked red head to identify the Turkey Vulture.

Stan's Notes: The naked head reduces the risk of feather fouling (picking up diseases) from contact with carcasses. It has a strong bill for tearing apart flesh. Unlike hawks and eagles, it has weak feet more suited for walking than grasping. One of the few birds with a developed sense of smell. Mostly mute, making only grunts and groans. Holds its wings in an upright V shape in flight. Teeters from wing tip to wing tip as it soars and hovers. Seen in trees with wings outstretched, sunning itself and drying after a rain.

in flight

juvenile

crests

drying

Double-crested Cormorant
Phalacrocorax auritus

Size:	31–35" (79–89 cm); up to 4⅓' wingspan
Male:	Large black waterbird with unusual blue eyes and a long, snake-like neck. Large gray bill, with yellow at the base and a hooked tip.
Female:	same as male
Juvenile:	lighter brown with a grayish chest and neck
Nest:	platform; male and female construct; 1 brood per year
Eggs:	3–4; bluish white without markings
Incubation:	25–29 days; female and male incubate
Fledging:	37–42 days; male and female feed the young
Migration:	non-migrator to partial in California
Food:	small fish, aquatic insects
Compare:	The Turkey Vulture (p. 53) is similar in size and also perches on branches with wings open to dry in sun, but it has a naked red head. American Coot (p. 43) is half the size and lacks the cormorant's long neck and long pointed bill.

Stan's Notes: Flocks fly in a large V or a line. Swims underwater to catch fish, holding its wings at its sides. This bird's outer feathers soak up water, but its body feathers don't. To dry off, it strikes an upright pose with wings outstretched, facing the sun. Gives grunts, pops and groans. Named "Double-crested" for the crests on its head, which are not often seen. "Cormorant" is a contraction from *corvus marinus*, meaning "crow" or "raven," and "of the sea."

male

female

Downy Woodpecker

Dryobates pubescens

Size: 6½" (15 cm)

Male: Small woodpecker with a white belly and black-and-white spotted wings. Red mark on the back of the head and a white stripe down the back. Short black bill.

Female: same as male but lacks the red mark

Juvenile: same as female, some with a red mark near the forehead

Nest: cavity with a round entrance hole; male and female excavate; 1 brood per year

Eggs: 3–5; white without markings

Incubation: 11–12 days; female incubates during the day, male incubates at night

Fledging: 20–25 days; male and female feed the young

Migration: non-migrator

Food: insects, seeds; visits seed and suet feeders

Compare: The Hairy Woodpecker (p. 65) is larger. Look for the Downy's shorter, thinner bill.

Stan's Notes: Abundant and widespread where trees are present. This is perhaps the most common woodpecker in the U.S. Stiff tail feathers help to brace it like a tripod as it clings to a tree. Like other woodpeckers, it has a long, barbed tongue to pull insects from tiny places. Mates drum on branches or hollow logs to announce territory, which is rarely larger than 5 acres (2 ha). Repeats a high-pitched "peek-peek" call. Nest cavity is wider at the bottom than at the top and is lined with fallen wood chips. Male performs most of the brooding. During winter, it will roost in a cavity. Doesn't breed in high elevations but often moves there in winter for food. Undulates in flight.

YEAR-ROUND

Black Phoebe
Sayornis nigricans

Size: 7" (18 cm)

Male: Black head, neck, breast and back with a white belly and undertail. Long narrow tail. Dark eyes, bill and legs. Can raise and lower its small crest.

Female: same as male

Juvenile: similar to adult, brown-to-tan wing bars

Nest: cup; female builds; 1–2 broods per year

Eggs: 3–6; white without markings

Incubation: 15–17 days; female incubates

Fledging: 14–21 days; female and male feed young

Migration: partial to non-migrator; will move around after breeding to find food

Food: insects

Compare: Distinctive black-and-white pattern makes identification easy. Watch for tail to pump up and down very quickly when perched. The male Vermilion Flycatcher (p. 393) is crimson and black. Say's Phoebe (p. 303) has a pale-orange belly and gray head.

Stan's Notes: Often seen in shrubby areas near water. Feeds mostly on insects near the surface of water. In the winter it feeds on insects near the ground. Like other flycatchers, the bird perches on thin branches, flies out to snatch a passing insect, and returns to perch. Pumps or bobs tail up and down quickly while perching. Male performs an aerial song and flight with a slow descent to attract a mate. Female builds shallow nest of mud, adhered to rocks or bridges, lined with hair and grass. Often uses same nest or location for several years.

male

female

Nuttall's Woodpecker
Dryobates nuttallii

YEAR-ROUND

Size: 7½" (19 cm)

Male: Mostly black and white barred woodpecker with a red cap and nape. Dull white breast and belly with black spots. Two black lines, one through the eyes and another extending from the bill, connect behind the cheek.

Female: same as male, but lacks a red spot on head and nape

Juvenile: similar to male, red spot closer to forehead

Nest: cavity; male and female build; 1–2 broods per year

Eggs: 3–6; white without markings

Incubation: 12–14 days; male and female incubate

Fledging: 24–28 days; male and female feed young

Migration: non-migrator

Food: insects, berries, seeds, tree sap

Compare: Downy (p. 57) and Hairy (p. 65) Woodpeckers have whiter breasts and bellies, a large white stripe on their backs, and males have smaller red markings on their heads.

Stan's Notes: Unique species to California. Prefers oak woodlands and moist areas with cottonwoods and willows. Creeps along a tree trunk, often boring a small hole to get to wood-boring insects. Diet consists of 80 percent insects. Pairs often stay together all year. Male defends territory. Usually excavates nest cavity in dead cottonwood, willow or alder tree near water. Nest is unlined. Male does the most incubating and brooding after the eggs hatch. Hybridization with Downy Woodpeckers often occurs where their ranges overlap.

61

male

female

Hairy Woodpecker
Leuconotopicus villous

Size: 9" (23 cm)

Male: Black-and-white woodpecker with a white belly. Black wings with rows of white spots. White stripe down the back. Long black bill. Red mark on the back of the head.

Female: same as male but lacks the red mark

Juvenile: grayer version of the female

Nest: cavity with an oval entrance hole; female and male excavate; 1 brood per year

Eggs: 3–6; white without markings

Incubation: 11–15 days; female incubates during the day, male incubates at night

Fledging: 28–30 days; male and female feed the young

Migration: non-migrator; moves around in winter to find food

Food: insects, nuts, seeds; comes to seed and suet feeders

Compare: Larger than Downy Woodpecker (p. 57) and has a longer bill. Nuttall's Woodpecker (p. 61) lacks a large white stripe on back.

Stan's Notes: A common bird in wooded backyards. Announces its arrival with a sharp chirp before landing on feeders. Responsible for eating many destructive forest insects. Uses its barbed tongue to extract insects from trees. Tiny, bristle-like feathers at the base of the bill protect the nostrils from wood dust. Drums on hollow logs, branches or stovepipes in spring to announce territory. Makes short flights from tree to tree. Prefers to excavate nest cavities in live aspen trees. Has a larger, more oval-shaped cavity entrance than that of the Downy Woodpecker.

male

female

Acorn Woodpecker
Melanerpes formicivorus

YEAR-ROUND

Size: 9" (22.5 cm)

Male: A black-and-white woodpecker with an all-black back and prominent white eyes. Red cap and nape of neck. White forehead and cheeks. White rump and tips of wings, seen in flight.

Female: same as male, but has a smaller bill and less red on head

Juvenile: similar to adult of the same sex

Nest: cavity; male and female excavate; 1 brood per year

Eggs: 3–7; white without markings

Incubation: 11–12 days; female and male incubate

Fledging: 30–32 days; female and male feed the young

Migration: non-migrator; moves around to find acorns

Food: nuts, fruit, insects, sap; comes to suet and seed feeders

Compare: Lewis's Woodpecker (p. 367) is larger and lacks the white on head and the red cap.

Stan's Notes: A woodpecker that depends upon acorns and other nuts for survival. Dead trees are very important to this species, as they are to all woodpeckers. Drills uniform holes in trees and telephone poles, where it wedges acorns and other nuts, storing them for later consumption. Unlike other woodpeckers, it lives and nests in small colonies. Colonies consist of up to 5 males, 1–2 females and up to 12 juveniles from previous years. All members help to raise the new young. This is a very vocal species, giving a loud, nasal "wheka-wheka-wheka" call.

male

female

YEAR-ROUND

Williamson's Sapsucker
Sphyrapicus thyroideus

Size: 9" (22.5 cm)

Male: More black than white with a red chin and bright-yellow belly. Bold white stripes just above and below the eyes. White rump and wing patches flash during flight.

Female: finely barred black-and-white back, a brown head, yellow belly and no wing patches

Juvenile: similar to female

Nest: cavity; male excavates; 1 brood per year

Eggs: 3–7; pale white without markings

Incubation: 12–14 days; male and female incubate

Fledging: 21–28 days; female and male feed young

Migration: non-migrator in California

Food: insects, tree sap; will visit feeders

Compare: Male Williamson's is similar to the Red-breasted Sapsucker (p. 63), which has white on the back and red on the head. Female Williamson's is similar to the Northern Flicker (p. 199), but the flicker has a gray head and brown-and-black back.

Stan's Notes: Largest sapsucker species with a striking difference between the male and female. Male drums early in spring to attract a mate and claim territory. Like the drumming of other sapsuckers, Williamson's drumming has an irregular cadence. Male excavates a new cavity each year, frequently in the same tree. Male does more incubating than the female. Occupies coniferous forests, foraging for insects and drilling uniform rows of holes from which tree sap oozes. Sap wells are nearly exclusively in conifers.

breeding

winter
p. 327

Black-bellied Plover
Pluvialis squatarola

WINTER

Size:	11–12" (28–30 cm)
Male:	Striking black-and-white breeding plumage. Belly, breast, sides, face and neck are black. Cap, nape of neck, and belly near tail are white. Black legs and bill.
Female:	less black on belly and breast than male
Juvenile:	grayer than adults, with much less black
Nest:	ground; male and female construct; 1 brood per year
Eggs:	3–4; pink or green with black-brown markings
Incubation:	26–27 days; male incubates during the day, female incubates at night
Fledging:	35–45 days; male feeds the young, the young learn quickly to feed themselves
Migration:	complete, to coastal California, Mexico and Central and South America
Food:	insects
Compare:	The Snowy Plover (p. 397) is smaller and lacks a black belly, face and chest.

Stan's Notes: Males perform a "butterfly" courtship flight to attract females. Female leaves male and young about 12 days after the eggs hatch. Breeds at age 3. Begins arriving in July and August (fall migration), leaves in April. Doesn't breed in California. During flight, in any plumage, displays a white rump and stripe on wings with black axillaries (armpits). Often darts across the ground to grab an insect and run. Can be very common on the beach during winter.

Yellow-billed Magpie
Pica nutalli

YEAR-ROUND

Size: 16½" (41.5 cm)

Male: A black head, neck and upper breast and back. White lower breast and belly. Wings and tail appear black but are an iridescent blue to green. Distinctive yellow bill.

Female: same as male

Juvenile: similar to adult

Nest: modified cup; female and male construct; 1 brood per year

Eggs: 4–7; olive with brown markings

Incubation: 16–18 days; female incubates

Fledging: 30–35 days; female and male feed young

Migration: non-migrator

Food: insects, fruit, carrion (road kill), seeds

Compare: Black-billed Magpie (p. 91) is larger and has a black bill and slightly longer tail.

Stan's Notes: A species found only in California (endemic). Very similar to the Black-billed Magpie in voice and appearance. Spends a lot of time on the ground. Walks and hops in search of insects or seeds. Three-quarters of diet is insects. Known to cache acorns and other foodstuffs in trees, presumably for later consumption. Slow, steady wing beats in flight, similar to the pattern of rowing a boat. Mated pairs raise wings, bow to each other and male feeds female. This behavior is believed to strengthen the pair bond. Male feeds female while she incubates. Pairs stay together throughout the year. Can be long-term mates. Usually seen with other Yellow-billeds, often family members. Nests in small colonies. Large domed nest is built high up, usually in a dense stand of trees.

female p.225

male

Lesser Scaup
Aythya affinis

YEAR-ROUND WINTER

Size: 16–17" (40–43 cm)

Male: Appears mostly black with bold white sides and a gray back. Chest and head look nearly black, but head appears purple with green highlights in direct sun. Bright-yellow eyes.

Female: overall brown with a dull-white patch at the base of a light-gray bill; yellow eyes

Juvenile: same as female

Nest: ground; female builds; 1 brood per year

Eggs: 8–14; olive-buff without markings

Incubation: 22–28 days; female incubates

Fledging: 45–50 days; female teaches the young to feed

Migration: complete, to California, Mexico, Central America and northern South America

Food: aquatic plants and insects

Compare: The male Ring-necked Duck (p. 83) has a bold white ring around its bill, a black back and lacks the bold white sides of the male Lesser Scaup. The male Blue-winged Teal (p. 221) is slightly smaller and has a bright white crescent-shaped mark at base of bill.

Stan's Notes: A common diving duck. Often seen in large flocks on lakes, ponds and sewage lagoons. Submerges completely to feed on the bottom (unlike dabbling ducks, which tip forward to reach the bottom). The male leaves the female when she starts incubating eggs. Egg quantity (clutch size) increases with the female's age. Has an interesting babysitting arrangement: groups of young (crèches) are tended by one to three adult females. A winter resident, it doesn't breed in most of California.

female
p. 231

male

WINTER

Hooded Merganser
Lophodytes cucullatus

Size: 16–19" (40–48 cm)

Male: Black-and-white with rust-brown sides. Crest "hood" raises to show a large white patch on each side of the head. Long, thin, black bill.

Female: brown and rust with ragged, rust-red "hair" and a long, thin, brown bill

Juvenile: similar to female

Nest: cavity; female lines an old woodpecker cavity or a nest box near water; 1 brood per year

Eggs: 10–12; white without markings

Incubation: 32–33 days; female incubates

Fledging: 71 days; female feeds the young

Migration: complete, to northwestern California

Food: small fish, aquatic insects, crustaceans (especially crayfish)

Compare: Male Bufflehead (p. 75) is smaller than Hooded Merganser and has white sides. The male Wood Duck (p. 371) is similar in size, but it has a green head. The white patch on the head and rust-brown sides distinguish the male Hoodie.

Stan's Notes: A small diving bird of shallow ponds, sloughs, lakes and rivers, usually in small groups. Quick, low flight across the water, with fast wingbeats. Male has a deep, rolling call. Female gives a hoarse quack. Nests in wooded areas. Female will lay some eggs in the nests of other Hooded Mergansers or Wood Ducks, resulting in 20–25 eggs in some nests. Rarely, she shares a nest, sitting with a Wood Duck.

female
p. 239

male

Common Goldeneye
Bucephala clangula

WINTER

Size: 18–20" (45–51 cm)

Male: Mostly white duck with a black back and a large, puffy green head. Large white spot on the face. Bright-golden eyes. Dark bill.

Female: Large dark-brown head with a gray body and a white collar. Bright-golden eyes and a yellow-tipped, dark bill.

Juvenile: same as female but has dark eyes

Nest: cavity; female lines an old woodpecker cavity; 1 brood per year

Eggs: 8–10; light green without markings

Incubation: 28–32 days; female incubates

Fledging: 56–59 days; female leads the young to food

Migration: complete, to California and Mexico

Food: aquatic plants, insects, fish, mollusks

Compare: Similar to the black-and-white male Lesser Scaup (p. 81), which is smaller. Look for the distinctive white spot on sides of the face and the golden eyes to identify the male goldeneye. Larger than breeding male Ruddy Duck (p. 217), which lacks the green head.

Stan's Notes: Known for the loud whistling sound produced by its wings during flight. During late winter and early spring, the male performs elaborate mating displays that include throwing his head back and calling a raspy note. The female will lay some of her eggs in other goldeneye nests or in the nests of other species (called egg dumping), causing some mothers to incubate as many as 30 eggs in a brood. Named for its bright-golden eyes. Winters in California where it finds open water.

in flight

juvenile

Black-crowned Night-Heron
Nycticorax nycticorax

YEAR-ROUND
SUMMER

Size: 22–27" (56–69 cm); up to 3½' wingspan

Male: A stocky, hunched and inactive heron with black back and crown, white belly and gray wings. Long dark bill and bright-red eyes. Short dull-yellow legs. Breeding adult has 2 long white plumes on crown.

Female: same as male

Juvenile: golden-brown head and back with white spots, streaked breast, yellow-orange eyes, brown bill

Nest: platform; female and male build; 1 brood per year

Eggs: 3–5; light blue without markings

Incubation: 24–26 days; female and male incubate

Fledging: 42–48 days; female and male feed the young

Migration: non-migrator to partial in California

Food: fish, aquatic insects

Compare: A perching Great Blue Heron (p. 353) looks twice the size of a Black-crowned. Look for a short-necked heron with a black back and crown.

Stan's Notes: A very secretive bird, this heron is most active near dawn and dusk (crepuscular). It hunts alone, but it nests in small colonies. Roosts in trees during the day. Often squawks if disturbed from the daytime roost. Often seen being harassed by other herons during the day.

93

soaring

SUMMER
MIGRATION
WINTER

Osprey
Pandion haliaetus

Size: 21–24" (53–61 cm); up to 5½' wingspan

Male: Large eagle-like bird with a white chest, belly and head. Dark eye line. Nearly black back. Black "wrist" marks on the wings. Dark bill.

Female: same as male but slightly larger and with a necklace of brown streaks

Juvenile: similar to adults, with a light-tan breast

Nest: platform on a raised wooden surface, man-made tower or tall dead tree; female and male build; 1 brood per year

Eggs: 2–4; white with brown markings

Incubation: 32–42 days; female and male incubate

Fledging: 48–58 days; male and female feed the young

Migration: complete, to southern California, Mexico and Central and South America

Food: fish

Compare: The juvenile Bald Eagle (p. 99) is brown with white speckles. The adult Bald Eagle has an all-white head and tail. Look for the white belly and dark eye line to identify the Osprey.

Stan's Notes: The only species in its family, and the only raptor that plunges into water feetfirst to catch fish. Always near water. Can hover for a few seconds before diving. Carries fish in a head-first position for better aerodynamics. Wings angle back in flight. Often harassed by Bald Eagles for its catch. Gives a high-pitched, whistle-like call, often calling in flight as a warning. Mates have a long-term pair bond. May not migrate to the same wintering grounds. Was nearly extinct but is now doing well.

soaring

juvenile

soaring
juvenile

YEAR-ROUND
WINTER

Bald Eagle
Haliaeetus leucocephalus

Size: 31–37" (79–94 cm); up to 7½' wingspan

Male: White head and tail contrast sharply with the dark-brown-to-black body and wings. Large, curved yellow bill and yellow feet.

Female: same as male but larger

Juvenile: dark brown with white speckles and spots on the body and wings; gray bill

Nest: massive platform, usually in a tree; female and male build; 1 brood per year

Eggs: 2–3; off-white without markings

Incubation: 34–36 days; female and male incubate

Fledging: 75–90 days; female and male feed the young

Migration: partial to non-migrator in California

Food: fish, carrion, birds (mainly ducks)

Compare: The Golden Eagle (p. 267) and Turkey Vulture (p. 53) lack the white head and white tail of adult Bald Eagle. The juvenile Golden Eagle (p. 267), with its white wrist marks and white base of tail, is similar to the juvenile Bald Eagle.

Stan's Notes: Nearly became extinct due to DDT poisoning and illegal killing. Returns to the same nest each year, adding more sticks and enlarging it to huge proportions, at times up to 1,000 pounds (450 kg). In their midair mating ritual, one eagle flips upside down and locks talons with another. Both tumble, then break apart to continue flight. Not uncommon for juveniles to perform this mating ritual even though they have not reached breeding age. Long-term pair bond but will switch mates when not successful at reproducing. Juveniles attain the white head and tail at 4–5 years of age. Winter resident except for a few scattered locations.

Blue-gray Gnatcatcher
Polioptila caerulea

YEAR-ROUND
SUMMER
MIGRATION

Size: 4" (10 cm)

Male: A light-blue-to-gray head, back, breast and wings, with a white belly. Black forehead and eyebrows. Prominent white eye-ring. Long black tail with a white undertail, often held cocked above the rest of body.

Female: same as male but grayer and lacking black on the head

Juvenile: similar to female

Nest: cup; female and male construct; 1 brood per year

Eggs: 4–5; pale blue with dark markings

Incubation: 10–13 days; female and male incubate

Fledging: 10–12 days; female and male feed the young

Migration: complete to non-migrator, to southern California, Mexico and Central America

Food: insects

Compare: The breeding male California Gnatcatcher (p. 279) has a black cap. Very active near the nest. Look for it flitting around upper branches in search of insects.

Stan's Notes: Found in a wide variety of scrublands in California. Listen for its wheezy call notes to help locate. A fun and easy bird to watch. Flicks its tail up and down and from side to side while calling. Like many open-woodland nesters, it is a common cowbird host. Returns to California by mid-April, with most leaving by late August. Although the population is abundant and widespread, it has been decreasing in the recent past.

Barn Swallow
Hirundo rustica

SUMMER
MIGRATION

Size: 7" (18 cm)

Male: Sleek swallow. Blue-black back, cinnamon belly and reddish-brown chin. White spots on a long, deeply forked tail.

Female: same as male but with a whitish belly

Juvenile: similar to adults, with a tan belly and chin, and shorter tail

Nest: cup; female and male build; 2 broods per year

Eggs: 4–5; white with brown markings

Incubation: 13–17 days; female incubates

Fledging: 18–23 days; female and male feed the young

Migration: complete, to South America

Food: insects (prefers beetles, wasps, flies)

Compare: The Tree Swallow (p. 107) has a white belly and chin and a notched tail. Cliff Swallow (p. 141) is smaller and lacks a distinctive, deeply forked tail.

Stan's Notes: Seen in wetlands, farms, suburban yards and parks. Of the seven swallow species regularly found in California, this is the only one with a deeply forked tail. Unlike other swallows, it rarely glides in flight. Usually flies low over land or water. Drinks as it flies, skimming water, or will sip water droplets on wet leaves. Bathes while flying through rain or sprinklers. Gives a twittering warble, followed by a mechanical sound. Builds a mud nest with up to 1,000 beak-loads of mud. Nests on barns and houses, under bridges and in other sheltered places. Often nests in colonies of 4–6 birds; sometimes nests alone.

female
p. 163

male

Blue Grosbeak
Passerina caerulea

SUMMER MIGRATION

Size: 7" (18 cm)

Male: Overall blue bird with 2 chestnut wing bars. Large gray-to-silver bill. Black around base of bill.

Female: overall brown with darker wings and tail, 2 tan wing bars, large gray-to-silver bill

Juvenile: similar to female

Nest: cup; female builds; 1–2 broods per year

Eggs: 3–6; pale blue without markings

Incubation: 11–12 days; female incubates

Fledging: 9–10 days; female and male feed the young

Migration: complete, to Mexico and Central America

Food: insects, seeds; will come to seed feeders

Compare: Male Lazuli Bunting (p. 105) has two bold white wing bars and a white belly. The male Mountain and Western Bluebirds (pp. 113 and 115) are the same size, but they lack the chestnut wing bars and oversize bill.

Stan's Notes: This grosbeak returns to California by early May. A bird of semi-open habitats, such as overgrown fields, riversides, woodland edges and fencerows. Visits seed feeders. The first-year males show only some blue, obtaining the full complement of blue feathers in the second winter. Frequently seen twitching and spreading its tail. It has expanded northward, with overall populations increasing over the past 30–40 years.

male

female

Western Bluebird
Sialia mexicana

YEAR-ROUND
WINTER

Size: 7" (18 cm)

Male: Deep blue head, neck, throat, back, wings and tail. Rusty-red chest and flanks.

Female: similar to male, only duller with a gray head

Juvenile: similar to female, with a speckled chest

Nest: cavity, old woodpecker cavity, wooden nest box; female builds; 1–2 broods per year

Eggs: 4–6; pale blue without markings

Incubation: 13–14 days; female incubates

Fledging: 22–23 days; female and male feed young

Migration: non-migrator to partial migrator in California

Food: insects, fruit

Compare: The Mountain Bluebird (p. 113) is similar but lacks the rusty-red breast. Male Lazuli Bunting (p. 105) is smaller and has white wing bars. Male Blue Grosbeak (p. 111) is the same size but has chestnut wing bars and an oversize bill.

Stan's Notes: Not as common as the Mountain Bluebird. Found in a variety of habitats, from agricultural land to clear-cuts. Requires a cavity for nesting. Competes with starlings for nest cavities. Like the Mountain Bluebird, it uses nest boxes, which are responsible for the stable populations. A courting male will fly in front of the female, spread his wings and tail, and perch next to her. Often goes in and out of its nest box or cavity as if to say, "Look inside." Male may offer food to the female to establish a pair bond.

Island
Scrub-Jay

California Scrub-Jay
Aphelocoma californica

YEAR-ROUND

Size: 11" (28 cm)

Male: Head, wings, tail and breast band are deep blue. Brownish patch on back. Chin, breast and belly are dull white. Very long tail.

Female: same as male

Juvenile: similar to adult, overall gray with light-blue wings and tail

Nest: cup; female and male build; 1 brood a year

Eggs: 3–6; pale green with red-brown markings

Incubation: 15–17 days; female incubates

Fledging: 18–20 days; female and male feed the young

Migration: non-migrator

Food: insects, seeds, fruit; comes to seed feeders

Compare: Same size as Steller's Jay (p. 117), but it lacks the all-black head and pointed crest.

Stan's Notes: A tame bird of urban areas that visits feeders. Island Scrub-Jay (see inset) is closely related, but found only on Santa Cruz Island. This species is darker blue and overall larger than the California Scrub-Jay. Forms a long-term pair bond. The male feeds the female before and during incubation. Young of a pair remain close by for up to a couple of years, helping parents raise subsequent siblings. Caches food by burying it for later consumption. Likely serves as a major distributor of oaks and pines by not returning to eat the seeds it buried. Was once called the Western Scrub-Jay. Now broken into two separates species, the California Scrub-Jay and the Woodhouse's Scrub-Jay. The California Scrub-Jay occurs in California, Washington and Oregon, while Woodhouse's is found in Idaho and other Rocky Mountain states.

YEAR-ROUND

Chestnut-backed Chickadee
Poecile rufescens

Size: 4¾" (12 cm)

Male: Rich, warm chestnut back and sides. Black crown and chin. White cheeks and sides of head. Gray wings and tail.

Female: same as male

Juvenile: same as adult

Nest: cavity; female and male build; 1–2 broods per year

Eggs: 5–7; white without markings

Incubation: 10–12 days; female incubates

Fledging: 13–16 days; female and male feed the young

Migration: non-migrator; moves around to find food

When Seen: year-round

Food: insects, seeds, fruit; comes to seed and suet feeders

Compare: Mountain Chickadee (p. 289) lacks Chestnut-backed's distinctive chestnut back.

Stan's Notes: The most colorful of all chickadees. Like the other chickadee species, the Chestnut-backed clings to branches upside down, looking for insects. During breeding, it is quiet and secretive. In winter it joins other birds such as kinglets, woodpeckers and other chickadees. Prefers humid coastal coniferous forests with hemlock and Tamarack. Builds a cavity nest 2–20 feet (up to 6 m) above the ground. Will use the same nest year after year. In late summer, some move to higher elevations and back down just before winter starts. Can be attracted to your yard with nest boxes. Comes to seed and suet feeders.

Chipping Sparrow

Spizella passerina

YEAR-ROUND
SUMMER
MIGRATION
WINTER

Size: 5" (13 cm)

Male: Small gray-brown sparrow with clear-gray chest. Rusty crown. White eyebrows and thin black eye line. Thin gray-black bill. Two faint wing bars.

Female: same as male

Juvenile: similar to adults, with streaking on the chest; lacks a rusty crown

Nest: cup; female builds; 2 broods per year

Eggs: 3–5; blue-green with brown markings

Incubation: 11–14 days; female incubates

Fledging: 10–12 days; female and male feed the young

Migration: complete to non-migrator in California

Food: insects, seeds; will come to ground feeders

Compare: The Lark Sparrow (p. 155) is larger and has a white chest and central spot. Song Sparrow (p. 135) and female House Finch (p. 131) have heavily streaked chests. Fox Sparrow (p. 161) is larger and lacks the rusty crown.

Stan's Notes: A common garden or yard bird, often seen feeding on dropped seeds beneath feeders. Gathers in large family groups to feed in preparation for migration. Migrates at night in flocks of 20–30 birds. The common name comes from the male's fast "chip" call. Often is just called Chippy. Builds nest low in dense shrubs and almost always lines it with animal hair. Comfortable with people, allowing you to approach closely before it flies away.

Pine Siskin

Spinus pinus

YEAR-ROUND WINTER

Size: 5" (13 cm)

Male: Small brown finch with heavy streaking on the back, breast and belly. Yellow wing bars. Yellow at the base of tail. Thin bill.

Female: similar to male, with less yellow

Juvenile: similar to adult, with a light-yellow tinge over the breast and chin

Nest: cup; female builds; 2 broods

Eggs: 3–4; greenish blue with brown markings

Incubation: 12–13 days; female incubates

Fledging: 14–15 days; female and male feed the young

Migration: non-migrator to partial migrator; moves around the United States in search of food

Food: seeds, insects; will come to seed feeders

Compare: Female House Finch (p. 131) lacks any yellow. The female American Goldfinch (p. 423) has white wing bars and lacks streaks. Look for the yellow wing bars to identify the Pine Siskin.

Stan's Notes: A nesting resident, it is usually considered a winter finch because it is more visible in the non-nesting season, when it gathers in flocks, moves around the state and visits bird feeders. Seen in flocks of up to 20 birds, often with other finch species. Will come to thistle feeders. Gives a series of high-pitched, wheezy calls. Also gives a wheezing twitter. Breeds in small groups. Builds nest toward the end of coniferous branches, where needles are dense, helping to conceal. Nests are often only a few feet apart. Male feeds the female during incubation. Juveniles lose the yellow tint by late summer of their first year.

male
p. 391

female

House Finch
Haemorhous mexicanus

YEAR-ROUND

Size: 5" (13 cm)

Female: Plain brown with heavy streaking on a white chest.

Male: red-to-orange face, throat, chest and rump, streaked belly and wings, brown cap, brown marking behind the eyes

Juvenile: similar to female

Nest: cup, occasionally in a cavity; female builds; 2 broods per year

Eggs: 4–5; pale blue, lightly marked

Incubation: 12–14 days; female incubates

Fledging: 15–19 days; female and male feed the young

Migration: non-migrator; will move around to find food

Food: seeds, fruit, leaf buds; visits seed feeders and feeders that offer grape jelly

Compare: Pine Siskin (p. 129) is similar but has yellow wing bars and a smaller bill. The female American Goldfinch (p. 423) has a clear chest and white wing bars.

Stan's Notes: Can be a common bird at feeders. A very social bird, visiting feeders in small flocks. Likes to nest in hanging flower baskets. Incubating female is fed by the male. Male sings a loud, cheerful warbling song. Historically it occurred from the Pacific Coast to the Rockies, with only a few reaching the eastern side. Now found throughout the country. Suffers from a disease that causes the eyes to crust, resulting in blindness and death.

House Wren
Troglodytes aedon

YEAR-ROUND
SUMMER
MIGRATION
WINTER

Size: 5" (13 cm)

Male: All-brown bird with lighter-brown markings on the wings and tail. Slightly curved brown bill. Often holds tail upward.

Female: same as male

Juvenile: same as adult

Nest: cavity; female and male line just about any nest cavity; 2 broods per year

Eggs: 4–6; tan with brown markings

Incubation: 10–13 days; female and male incubate

Fledging: 12–15 days; female and male feed the young

Migration: complete, to California and Mexico; non-migrator in parts of California

Food: insects, spiders, snails

Compare: The Bewick's Wren (p. 143) is slightly larger and has white eyebrows. Canyon Wren (p. 145) is larger and has a white throat and breast.

Stan's Notes: A prolific songster. During the mating season, sings from dawn to dusk. Seen in brushy yards, parks and woodlands and along forest edges. Easily attracted to a nest box. In spring, the male chooses several prospective nesting cavities and places a few small twigs in each. The female inspects all of them and finishes constructing the nest in the cavity of her choice. She fills the cavity with short twigs and then lines a small depression at the back with pine needles and grass. She often has trouble fitting longer twigs through the entrance hole and tries many different directions and approaches until she is successful.

Song Sparrow
Melospiza melodia

YEAR-ROUND

Size:	5–6" (13–15 cm)
Male:	Common brown sparrow with heavy dark streaks on the chest coalescing into a central dark spot.
Female:	same as male
Juvenile:	similar to adults, with a finely streaked chest; lacks a central dark spot
Nest:	cup; female builds; 2 broods per year
Eggs:	3–4; blue to green, with red-brown markings
Incubation:	12–14 days; female incubates
Fledging:	9–12 days; female and male feed the young
Migration:	non-migrator in California
Food:	insects, seeds; only rarely comes to ground feeders with seeds
Compare:	Similar to other brown sparrows. Look for the heavily streaked chest with a central dark spot to help identify the Song Sparrow.

Stan's Notes: There are many subspecies of this bird, but the dark spot in the center of the chest appears in every variety. A constant songster, repeating its loud, clear song every few minutes. The song varies from region to region but has the same basic structure. Sings from thick shrubs to defend a small territory, beginning with three notes and finishing up with a trill. A ground feeder, it will "double-scratch" with both feet at the same time to expose seeds. When the female builds a new nest for a second brood, the male often takes over feeding the first brood. Unlike many other sparrow species, Song Sparrows rarely flock together. A common host of the Brown-headed Cowbirds.

male
p. 291

female

Oregon
female

Dark-eyed Junco
Junco hyemalis

YEAR-ROUND
WINTER

Size: 5½" (14 cm)

Female: A plump, dark-eyed bird with a tan-to-brown chest, head and back. White belly. Ivory-to-pink bill. White outer tail feathers appear like a white V in flight.

Male: round bird with gray plumage

Juvenile: similar to female, with streaking on the breast and head

Nest: cup; female and male build; 2 broods per year

Eggs: 3–5; white with reddish-brown markings

Incubation: 12–13 days; female incubates

Fledging: 10–13 days; male and female feed the young

Migration: partial to non-migrator in California

Food: seeds, insects; visits ground and seed feeders

Compare: Rarely confused with any other bird. Look for the ivory-to-pink bill and small flocks feeding beneath seed feeders to help identify the female Dark-eyed Junco.

Stan's Notes: This bird is one of the most numerous wintering birds in the state. A common year-round resident in parts of California. Spends winters in foothills and plains after snowmelt, returning to higher elevations for nesting. Adheres to a rigid social hierarchy, with dominant birds chasing the less dominant birds. Look for the white outer tail feathers flashing in flight. Often seen in small flocks on the ground, where it uses its feet to simultaneously "double-scratch" to expose seeds and insects. Eats many weed seeds. Nests in a wide variety of wooded habitats in April and May. Several sub-species of Dark-eyed Junco were previously considered to be separate species (see lower inset).

female

male
p. 105

Lazuli Bunting
Passerina amoena

SUMMER
MIGRATION

Size: 5½" (14 cm)

Female: Overall grayish brown with a warm brown chest, light wash of blue on wings and tail, gray throat and light-gray belly. Two narrow white wing bars.

Male: turquoise-blue head, neck, back and tail, cinnamon breast, white belly, 2 bold white wing bars

Juvenile: similar to adult of the same sex

Nest: cup; female builds; 2–3 broods per year

Eggs: 3–5; pale blue without markings

Incubation: 11–13 days; female incubates

Fledging: 10–12 days; female and male feed the young

Migration: complete, to Mexico

Food: insects, seeds

Compare: Similar to the female Blue Grosbeak (p. 163), which is overall darker and has tan wing bars. Female Western (p. 115) and Mountain (p. 113) Bluebirds are larger and have much more blue than the female Lazuli Bunting.

Stan's Notes: More common in shrublands in California. Doesn't like dense forests. Strong association with water, such as rivers and streams. Gathers in small flocks and tends to move up in elevations after breeding to hunt for insects and look for seeds. Has increased in population and expanded its range over the last century. Males sing from short shrubs and scrubby areas to attract females. Rarely perches on tall trees. Each male has his own unique combination of notes to produce his own song.

Cliff Swallow

Petrochelidon pyrrhonota

SUMMER
MIGRATION

Size: 5½" (14 cm)

Male: Uniquely patterned swallow with a dark back, wings and cap. Distinctive tan-to-rust rump, cheeks and forehead.

Female: same as male

Juvenile: similar to adult, lacks distinct patterning

Nest: gourd-shaped, made of mud; male and female build; 1–2 broods per year

Eggs: 4–6; pale white with brown markings

Incubation: 14–16 days; male and female incubate

Fledging: 21–24 days; female and male feed young

Migration: complete, to South America

Food: insects

Compare: Barn Swallow (p. 109) is larger and has a distinctive, deeply forked tail and blue back and wings.

Stan's Notes: A common and widespread swallow species in the state during summer and migration. Common around bridges (especially bridges over water) and rural housing (especially in open country near cliffs). Builds a gourd-shaped nest with a funnel-like entrance pointing down. A colony nester, with many nests lined up beneath building eaves or cliff overhangs. Will carry balls of mud up to a mile to construct its nest. Many in the colony return to the same nest site each year. Not unusual to have two broods per season. If the number of nests underneath eaves becomes a problem, wait until the young have left the nests to hose off the mud.

Canyon Wren

Catherpes mexicanus

Size: 5¾" (14.5 cm)

Male: Chestnut back, wings, belly and tail. Gray head and nape of neck. A distinctive white throat and chest. Long downward-curving bill. Tail often cocked up.

Female: same as male

Juvenile: similar to adult

Nest: crevice; male and female build; 1–2 broods per year

Eggs: 4–6; white with light-brown markings

Incubation: 14–16 days; female and male incubate

Fledging: 14–18 days; female and male feed young

Migration: non-migrator to partial; will move around to find food

Food: insects

Compare: Rock Wren (p. 147) is slightly larger and tends to be more grayish, with white chin not as prominent. House Wren (p. 133) is slightly smaller and lacks the large bill of the Canyon Wren.

Stan's Notes: An active wren, spending its entire life among rocks and cliffs. Prefers steep-sided canyons, hence its common name. Maintains winter territories, usually around running water, to hunt for winter-active insects. Territories are up to 2 acres (1 ha) in size. Nests are attached to rocks within crevices that usually have some kind of rock covering. May reuse the nest from year to year.

Rock Wren
Salpinctes obsoletus

YEAR-ROUND
WINTER

Size: 6" (15 cm)

Male: Overall grayish brown with tinges of buffy brown on tail and wings. Gray back, often finely speckled with white. Belly and breast are light tan.

Female: same as male

Juvenile: similar to adult

Nest: crevice; male and female build; 1–2 broods per year

Eggs: 4–8; white with light-brown markings

Incubation: 14–16 days; female and male incubate

Fledging: 14–18 days; female and male feed young

Migration: non-migrator in most of California

Food: insects

Compare: Canyon Wren (p. 145) is slightly smaller, mostly chestnut brown, and has a much larger and down-curved bill. House Wren (p. 133) is slightly smaller and lacks Rock Wren's white speckles on its back.

Stan's Notes: Consistently uses open sunny piles of broken rocks (scree) and rock debris at cliff bases (talus slopes) for nesting. Often builds a small runway of flat stones leading up to the nest, which is usually in a rock crevice. Lives in close association with Canyon Wrens, which use steep-sided canyons for nesting. Known to also nest on prairies, where it uses dirt banks instead of rock piles. Begins nesting in May, with the female doing most of the incubating and the male feeding the female during incubation.

winter p. 299

breeding

Least Sandpiper
Calidris minutilla

Size: 6" (15 cm)

Male: Breeding plumage has a golden-brown head and back and a white belly. Dull-yellow legs. White eyebrows and a short, down-curved black bill.

Female: same as male

Juvenile: similar to winter adult but buff-brown and lacks the breast band

Nest: ground; male and female construct; 1 brood per year

Eggs: 3–4; olive with dark markings

Incubation: 19–23 days; male and female incubate

Fledging: 25–28 days; male and female feed the young

Migration: complete, to parts of California, Mexico and Central America

Food: aquatic and terrestrial insects, seeds

Compare: The smallest of sandpipers. Often confused with breeding Western Sandpiper (p. 153). Look for Least Sandpiper's yellow legs to differentiate it from other tiny sandpipers. The short, thin down-curved bill also helps to identify.

Stan's Notes: A winter resident in parts of California. This is a tiny, tame sandpiper that can be approached without scaring. It is the smallest of peeps (sandpipers), nesting on the tundra in northern regions of Canada and Alaska. Prefers the grassy flats of saltwater and freshwater ponds. Its yellow legs can be hard to see in water, poor light or when covered with mud.

151

winter p. 301

breeding

Western Sandpiper
Calidris mauri

MIGRATION
WINTER

Size: 6½" (16 cm)

Male: Breeding has a bright rust-brown crown, ear patch and back and a white chin and chest. Black legs. Narrow bill that droops near tip.

Female: same as male

Juvenile: similar to breeding adult; bright buff-brown on the back only

Nest: ground; male and female construct; 1 brood per year

Eggs: 2–4; light brown with dark markings

Incubation: 20–22 days; male and female incubate

Fledging: 19–21 days; male and female feed the young

Migration: complete, to coastal California, Mexico and Central America

Food: aquatic and terrestrial insects

Compare: Breeding Least Sandpiper (p. 151) lacks the bright rust-brown cap, ear patch and back. Least Sandpiper has yellow legs. Look for Western's longer bill that droops slightly at the tip.

Stan's Notes: A winter resident along coastal California and a long-distance migrant. Nests on the ground in large "loose" colonies on the tundra of northern coastal Alaska. Adults leave their breeding grounds several weeks before the young. Some obtain their breeding plumage before leaving California in spring. Feeds on insects at the water's edge, sometimes immersing its head. Young leave the nest (precocial) within a few hours after hatching. Female leaves and the male tends the hatchlings.

Lark Sparrow
Chondestes grammacus

YEAR-ROUND
SUMMER
MIGRATION
WINTER

Size: 6½" (16 cm)

Male: All-brown bird with unique rust-red, white and black head pattern. A white breast with a central black spot. Gray rump and white edges to gray tail, as seen in flight.

Female: same as male

Juvenile: similar to adult, but no rust-red on head

Nest: cup, on the ground; female builds; 1 brood per year

Eggs: 3–6; pale white with brown markings

Incubation: 10–12 days; male and female incubate

Fledging: 10–12 days; female and male feed young

Migration: non-migrator to complete in California

Food: seeds, insects

Compare: The White-crowned Sparrow (p. 159) lacks the Lark Sparrow's rust-red pattern on the head and central spot on a white chest. Chipping Sparrow (p. 127) has a similar rusty color on head, but it is smaller and lacks Lark Sparrow's white breast and central spot.

Stan's Notes: One of the larger sparrow species and one of the best songsters, also well known for its courtship strutting, chasing and lark-like flight pattern (rapid wingbeats with tail spread). A bird of open fields, pastures and prairies, found almost anywhere. Very common during migration, when large flocks congregate. Will use nest for several years if first brood is successful.

Wrentit

Chamaea fasciata

YEAR-ROUND

Size: 6½" (16 cm)

Male: A small bird, all-brown to gray, with a long tail often held pointing upward (cocked). Obvious pale eyes. Lightly streaked breast.

Female: same as male

Juvenile: paler version of adult

Nest: cup; the male and female build; 1–2 broods per year

Eggs: 3–5; pale green to blue without markings

Incubation: 15–16 days; female and male incubate

Fledging: 15–16 days; female and male feed young

Migration: non-migrator

Food: insects, fruit

Compare: The Mountain Chickadee (p. 289) and the Chestnut-backed Chickadee (p. 123) are smaller and have black markings, which the Wrentit lacks. Look for the obvious long tail of Wrentit to help identify.

Stan's Notes: A bird of the chaparral and brushy areas along the coast. This bird reaches its northernmost limits in Oregon. Adults feed on a nearly fifty-fifty mix of berries and insects; the young, however, are fed a strictly insect diet. Often heard more than seen, giving a bouncing Ping-Pong ball type of song. Mates for life, rarely leaving its small territory of about an acre in size. Wrentits are not a type of wren or European tit, but belong to a separate family (Timaliidae). Doesn't have any close relatives in North America.

Fox Sparrow
Passerella iliaca

YEAR-ROUND
SUMMER
MIGRATION
WINTER

Size: 7" (18 cm)

Male: A plump, brown sparrow with a gray head, back and rump. White chest and belly with rusty brown streaks. Rusty tail and wings.

Female: same as male

Juvenile: same as adult

Nest: cup; female builds; 2 broods per year

Eggs: 2–4; pale green with reddish markings

Incubation: 12–14 days; female incubates

Fledging: 10–11 days; male and female feed the young

Migration: complete to non-migrator in California

Food: seeds, insects; comes to ground feeders

Compare: The Spotted Towhee (p. 31) is found in similar habitats, but the male towhee has a black head and both male and female have white bellies.

Stan's Notes: One of the largest sparrows. Often alone or in small groups. Found in shrubby areas, open fields and backyards. Comes to ground feeders and often seen underneath seed feeders during migration, searching for seeds and insects. Like a chicken, it will "double-scratch" with both feet at the same time to look for food. Gives a series of rich notes lasting 2–3 seconds, usually singing from a perch hidden in a shrub. The common name "Sparrow" comes from the Anglo-Saxon word *spearwa*, meaning "flutterer," and applies to any small bird. "Fox" refers to its rusty color. Appears in several color variations, depending on the part of the country. Fox Sparrows in western states have gray heads and backs.

male
p. 111

female

Blue Grosbeak
Passerina caerulea

SUMMER
MIGRATION

Size: 7" (18 cm)

Female: Overall brown with darker wings and tail. Two tan wing bars. Large gray-to-silver bill.

Male: blue bird with 2 chestnut wing bars; large gray-to-silver bill; black around base of bill

Juvenile: similar to female

Nest: cup; female builds; 1–2 broods per year

Eggs: 3–6; pale blue without markings

Incubation: 11–12 days; female incubates

Fledging: 9–10 days; female and male feed the young

Migration: complete, to Mexico and Central America

Food: insects, seeds; will come to seed feeders

Compare: The female Lazuli Bunting (p. 139) is similar, but it has two narrow white wing bars and is lighter color overall.

Stan's Notes: This grosbeak returns to California by early May. A bird of semi-open habitats such as overgrown fields, riversides, woodland edges and fencerows. Visits seed feeders. Often seen twitching and spreading its tail. The first-year males show only some blue, obtaining the full complement of blue feathers in the second winter. It has expanded northward, and its overall populations have increased over the past 30–40 years.

female

male

YEAR-ROUND
MIGRATION

Horned Lark
Eremophila alpestris

Size: 7–8" (18–20 cm)

Male: Tan to brown with black markings on the face. Black necklace and bill. Pale-yellow chin. Two tiny feather "horns" on the top of the head, sometimes hard to see. Dark tail with white outer tail feathers, seen in flight.

Female: duller than male; less noticeable "horns"

Juvenile: lacks a yellow chin and black markings; does not develop "horns" until the second year

Nest: ground; female builds; 2–3 broods per year

Eggs: 3–4; gray with brown markings

Incubation: 11–12 days; female incubates

Fledging: 9–12 days; female and male feed the young

Migration: non-migrator in most of California

Food: seeds, insects

Compare: Western Meadowlark (p. 441) is larger and has a yellow breast and belly. Look for the black markings by the eyes and the black necklace to identify the Horned Lark.

Stan's Notes: The only true lark native to North America. A bird of open ground. Common in rural areas; often seen in large flocks. The population increased in North America over the past century as more land was cleared for farming. Male performs a fluttering courtship flight high in the air while singing a high-pitched song. Female performs a fluttering distraction display when the nest is disturbed. Starts breeding early in the year. Able to renest about a week after the brood fledges. Moves around in winter to find food. "Lark" comes from the Middle English *laverock*, or "a lark."

male
p. 25

female

Brown-headed Cowbird

Molothrus ater

YEAR-ROUND
SUMMER

Size: 7½" (19 cm)

Female: Dull brown with no obvious markings. Pointed, sharp gray bill. Dark eyes.

Male: glossy black with a chocolate-brown head

Juvenile: similar to female but with dull-gray plumage and a streaked chest

Nest: no nest; lays eggs in the nests of other birds

Eggs: 5–7; white with brown markings

Incubation: 10–13 days; host birds incubate the eggs

Fledging: 10–11 days; host birds feed the young

Migration: non-migrator to partial in California

Food: insects, seeds; will come to seed feeders

Compare: The female Red-winged Blackbird (p. 181) has white eyebrows and heavy streaking. European Starling (p. 27) has speckles and a shorter tail. The pointed gray bill helps to identify the female Brown-headed Cowbird.

Stan's Notes: Cowbirds are members of the blackbird family. Of approximately 750 species of parasitic birds worldwide, this is the only parasitic bird in the state. Brood parasites lay their eggs in the nests of other birds, leaving the host birds to raise their young. Cowbirds are known to have laid their eggs in the nests of over 200 species of birds. While some birds reject cowbird eggs, most incubate them and raise the young, even to the exclusion of their own. Look for warblers and other birds feeding young birds twice their own size. Named "cowbird" for its habit of following bison and cattle herds to feed on insects flushed up by the animals.

1 year
old

Cedar Waxwing
Bombycilla cedrorum

YEAR-ROUND
WINTER

Size: 7½" (19 cm)

Male: Sleek-looking, gray-to-brown bird. Pointed crest, bandit-like mask and light-yellow belly. Bold-yellow tip of tail. Red wing tips look like they were dipped in red wax.

Female: same as male

Juvenile: grayish with a heavily streaked breast; lacks the sleek look, black mask and red wing tips

Nest: cup; female and male construct; 1 brood per year, occasionally 2

Eggs: 4–6; pale blue with brown markings

Incubation: 10–12 days; female incubates

Fledging: 14–18 days; female and male feed the young

Migration: complete migrator in California; non-migrator in far northwest California; moves around to find food

Food: cedar cones, fruit, insects

Compare: Look for the red wing tips, yellow-tipped tail and black mask to identify the Cedar Waxwing.

Stan's Notes: The name is derived from its red, wax-like wing tips and preference for the small, berry-like cones of the cedar. Seen in flocks, moving around from area to area looking for berries. Feeds on insects during summer, before berries are abundant. Wanders during winter, searching for food supplies. Spends most of its time at the top of tall trees. Listen for the high-pitched "sreee" whistling sound it constantly makes while perched or in flight. Obtains the mask after the first year and red wing tips after the second year. Usually a winter resident

winter

breeding

Spotted Sandpiper
Actitis macularius

YEAR-ROUND
SUMMER
MIGRATION
WINTER

Size: 8" (20 cm)

Male: Olive-brown back with black spots on a white chest and belly. White line over eyes. Long, dull-yellow legs. Long bill. Winter plumage lacks spots on the chest and belly.

Female: same as male

Juvenile: similar to winter plumage, with a darker bill

Nest: ground; male builds; 2 broods per year

Eggs: 3–4; brownish with brown markings

Incubation: 20–24 days; male incubates

Fledging: 17–21 days; male feeds the young

Migration: complete migrator, to southern California, Mexico, Central and South America; non-migrator in parts of California

Food: aquatic insects

Compare: Killdeer (p. 197) has 2 black neck bands. Look for the black spots on the chest and belly and the bobbing tail to help identify the breeding Spotted Sandpiper.

Stan's Notes: One of the few shorebirds that will dive underwater when pursued. Able to fly straight up out of the water. Holds wings in a cup-like arc in flight, rarely lifting them above a horizontal plane. Walks as if delicately balanced. When standing, constantly bobs its tail. Gives a rapid series of "weet-weet-weet" calls when frightened and flying away. Female mates with multiple males and lays eggs in up to five nests. Male does all of the nest building, incubating and childcare without any help from the female. Lacks black spots on the chest and belly in winter.

winter
p. 307

breeding

WINTER

Sanderling
Calidris alba

Size: 8" (20 cm)

Male: Breeding adult (April to August) has a rusty head, chest and back with white belly. Black legs and bill.

Female: same as male

Juvenile: spotty black on the head and back, a white belly, black legs and bill

Nest: ground; male builds; 1–2 broods per year

Eggs: 3–4; greenish olive with brown markings

Incubation: 24–30 days; male and female incubate

Fledging: 16–17 days; female and male feed the young

Migration: complete, to coastal California Mexico and Central and South America

Food: insects

Compare: Spotted Sandpiper (p. 173) is the same size as Sanderling, but the breeding Spotted Sandpiper has black spots on its chest.

Stan's Notes: Very common shorebird in the state. Can be seen in groups on sandy beaches, running out with each retreating wave to feed. Look for a flash of white on the wings when it is in flight. Sometimes a female will mate with several males (polyandry), which results in males and the female incubating separate nests. Both sexes perform a distraction display if threatened. Nests on the Arctic tundra. Rests by standing on one leg (see inset) and tucking the other leg into its belly feathers. Often hops away on one leg, moving away from pedestrians on the beach. Surveys show a greater than 80 percent decline in numbers since the 1970s. Seen in breeding plumage from August to April.

YEAR-ROUND

Cactus Wren
Campylorhynchus brunneicapillus

Size: 8½" (22 cm)

Male: Large round-bodied wren with a chestnut-brown crown and a long tail. Many dark spots on upper breast to throat, often forming a central dark patch. Bold white eyebrows. Large, slightly downward-curving bill.

Female: same as male

Juvenile: similar to adult, shorter bill, lacks a spotty dark patch on breast

Nest: covered cup, domed or ball-shaped; female and male build; 2–3 broods per year

Eggs: 3–4; pale white to pink with brown marks

Incubation: 14–16 days; female incubates

Fledging: 19–23 days; female and male feed young

Migration: non-migrator

Food: insects, fruit, seeds; comes to seed feeders and water elements

Compare: Sage Thrasher (p. 311) is gray and lacks a down-curving bill. Look for the Cactus Wren's prominent white eyebrows to help identify.

Stan's Notes: Our largest wren. Backyard bird with a loud "krr-krr-krr-krr-krr" or "cha-cha-cha-cha" call. Male crouches, extends wings, fans tail and growls to female during courtship. Pairs stay together all year, defending territory. Builds a large nest usually in cholla or other cactus, lining the chamber with grasses and feathers. Male builds another nest while female incubates first clutch of eggs. After the last brood fledges, roosts in nest during non-breeding season.

female

male
p. 35

Tricolored Blackbird
Agelaius tricolor

YEAR-ROUND

Size:	9" (22.5 cm)
Female:	Overall dark brown with a gray chin and breast, a pointed dark bill and black legs. Dark reddish-brown eyes.
Male:	black with red and white shoulder patches (epaulets), pointed dark bill, dark reddish-brown eyes
Juvenile:	similar to female, but not as brown
Nest:	cup; female builds; 2 broods per year
Eggs:	3–4; pale green with brown markings
Incubation:	11–13 days; female incubates
Fledging:	11–14 days; female and male feed young
Migration:	non-migrator to partial migrator; will move around to find food
Food:	insects, seeds, grain; visits ground feeders
Compare:	The female Red-winged Blackbird (p. 181) is darker brown with reddish tones.

Stan's Notes: Blackbird species found mainly in California. Very closely related to Red-winged Blackbirds. Tricolored usually has a smaller bill than Red-winged. Flocks with Red-wingeds and other blackbirds during winter, moving around to find food and nesting colonies. Sometimes moves from one area to another for unknown reasons. Tricoloreds and Red-wingeds have some of the highest nesting densities of any bird species, with some colonies in the tens of thousands. Like the Red-winged, it nests in shallow freshwater marshes. Builds nest from woven sedges, grasses and other green plants. Attaches nest to upright cattail stems and lines it with finer plant fibers. Young are fed mainly insects.

California Towhee

Melozone crissalis

YEAR-ROUND

Size: 9" (22.5 cm)

Male: Overall light brown to gray with faint dark streaks. Lighter brown throat. Rusty brown just under base of tail. Long tail. Short bill.

Female: same as male

Juvenile: similar to adult

Nest: cup; female builds; 1–2 broods per year

Eggs: 2–6; pale blue with dark markings

Incubation: 11–14 days; female incubates

Fledging: 12–14 days; female and male feed young

Migration: non-migrator

Food: seeds, insects, fruit; visits ground feeders

Compare: Larger than Green-tailed Towhee (p. 365), which has a rusty-red cap and bright white chin and throat. The female Spotted Towhee (p. 31) is smaller with rusty-red sides and a white chest and belly.

Stan's Notes: A stocky bird that tends to remain in or near heavy brush or shrubs, but is common in suburban areas. Comes out in the open to feed. Dashes back at any disturbance. Usually seen on the ground foraging for seeds and insects. Comes to seeds on the ground scattered under a backyard feeder. Often seen in pairs and can be very tame in some places. Until recently, California Towhee and Canyon Towhee (not shown) were one species, called Brown Towhee. California Towhee is found only in California and in Baja California, Mexico. The Canyon Towhee is found in Arizona, New Mexico and Texas. Their ranges rarely overlap.

Burrowing Owl
Athene cunicularia

YEAR-ROUND
SUMMER

Size:	9–10" (24 cm); up to 2' wingspan
Male:	Brown owl with bold white spots and a white belly. Yellow eyes. Very long legs.
Female:	same as male
Juvenile:	same as adult, but belly is brown
Nest:	cavity, former underground mammal den; female and male line den; 1 brood per year
Eggs:	6–11; white without markings
Incubation:	26–30 days; female incubates
Fledging:	25–28 days; female and male feed young
Migration:	non-migrator to partial in California
Food:	insects, mammals, lizards, birds
Compare:	Western Screech-Owl (p. 315) is slightly smaller and has ear tufts. Great Horned Owl (p. 255) is more than twice the size of Burrowing and has feather tuft "horns." Burrowing spends most of its time on the ground, unlike the tree-loving Great Horned.

Stan's Notes: An owl of fields, open backyards, golf courses and airports. Nests in large family units or in small colonies. Takes over the underground dens of mammals, occasionally widening its den by kicking dirt backward. Lines den with cow pies, horse dung, grass and feathers. Some people have had success attracting these owls to their backyards by creating artificial dens. Often seen during the day, standing or sleeping around den entrance. Male brings food to incubating female, often moving family to a new den when young are just a few weeks old. Will bob head up and down while doing deep knee bends when agitated or threatened.

191

in flight

juvenile

male

female

in-flight
juvenile

American Kestrel
Falco sparverius

YEAR-ROUND

Size: 9–11" (23–28 cm); up to 2' wingspan

Male: Rust-brown back and tail. White breast with dark spots. Two vertical black lines on a white face. Blue-gray wings. Wide black band with a white edge on the tip of a rusty tail.

Female: similar to male but slightly larger, with rust-brown wings and dark bands on the tail

Juvenile: same as adult of the same sex

Nest: cavity; does not build a nest; 1 brood per year

Eggs: 4–5; white with brown markings

Incubation: 29–31 days; male and female incubate

Fledging: 30–31 days; female and male feed the young

Migration: non-migrator in California

Food: insects, small mammals and birds, reptiles

Compare: Similar to other falcons. Look for two vertical black stripes on the kestrel's face. No other small bird of prey has a rusty back and tail.

Stan's Notes: An unusual raptor because the sexes look different (dimorphic). Due to its small size, this falcon was once called a Sparrow Hawk. Hovers near roads, then dives for prey. Watch for it to pump its tail after landing on a perch. Perches nearly upright. Eats many grasshoppers. Adapts quickly to a wooden nest box. Can be extremely vocal, giving a loud series of high-pitched calls. Ability to see ultraviolet (UV) light helps it locate mice and other prey by their urine, which glows bright yellow in UV light.

male
p. 39

female

Yellow-headed Blackbird
Xanthocephalus xanthocephalus

YEAR-ROUND
SUMMER
MIGRATION
WINTER

Size: 9–11" (23–28 cm)

Female: Large brown bird with a dull-yellow head and chest. Slightly smaller than the male.

Male: black bird with a lemon-yellow head, breast and nape of neck, black mask, gray bill, and white wing patches

Juvenile: similar to female

Nest: cup; female builds; 2 broods per year

Eggs: 3–5; greenish white with brown markings

Incubation: 11–13 days; female incubates

Fledging: 9–12 days; female feeds the young

Migration: complete, to parts of California and Mexico

Food: insects, seeds; will come to ground feeders

Compare: Female Red-winged Blackbird (p. 181) is smaller and has white eyebrows and heavy streaking. Look for the dull-yellow head to help identify the female Yellow-headed.

Stan's Notes: Found around marshes, wetlands and lakes. Nests in deep water, unlike its cousin, the Red-winged Blackbird, which prefers shallow water. Usually heard before seen. Gives a raspy, low, metallic-sounding call. The male is the only large blackbird with a bright-yellow head. He gives an impressive mating display, flying with his head drooped and feet and tail pointing down while steadily beating his wings. Young keep low and out of sight for up to three weeks before they start to fly. Migrates in large flocks of as many as 200 birds, often with Red-winged Blackbirds and Brown-headed Cowbirds. Flocks of mainly males return in early April; females return later. Most colonies consist of 20–100 nests.

Killdeer
Charadrius vociferus

YEAR-ROUND

Size: 11" (28 cm)

Male: Upland shorebird with 2 black bands around the neck, like a necklace. Brown back and white belly. Bright reddish-orange rump, visible in flight.

Female: same as male

Juvenile: similar to adults, with a single neck band

Nest: ground; male scrapes; 2 broods per year

Eggs: 3–5; tan with brown markings

Incubation: 24–28 days; male and female incubate

Fledging: 25 days; male and female lead their young to food

Migration: non-migrator in California

Food: insects, worms, snails

Compare: The Spotted Sandpiper (p. 173) is found around water but lacks the 2 neck bands of the Killdeer.

Stan's Notes: Technically classified as a shorebird but lives in dry habitats instead of the shore. Often found in vacant fields, gravel pits, driveways, wetland edges or along railroad tracks. The only shorebird that has two black neck bands. Known to fake a broken wing to draw intruders away from the nest; once the nest is safe, the parent will take flight. Nests are just a slight depression in a dry area and are often hard to see. Hatchlings look like miniature adults walking on stilts. Soon after hatching, the young follow their parents around and peck for insects. Gives a loud and distinctive "kill-deer" call. Migrates in small flocks.

male

red-shafted
female

Northern Flicker

Colaptes auratus

YEAR-ROUND
WINTER

Size: 12" (30 cm)

Male: Brown and black with a red mustache and black necklace. Speckled chest. Gray head with a brown cap. Large white rump patch, seen only when flying.

Female: same as male but without a red mustache

Juvenile: same as adult of the same sex

Nest: cavity; female and male excavate; 1 brood per year

Eggs: 5–8; white without markings

Incubation: 11–14 days; female and male incubate

Fledging: 25–28 days; female and male feed the young

Migration: non-migrator to partial in California; moves around in winter

Food: insects (especially ants and beetles); comes to suet feeders

Compare: Female Williamson's Sapsucker (p. 69) has a finely barred back with a yellow belly and lacks flicker's black spots on chest and belly. Look for Flicker's speckled breast and gray head to help identify.

Stan's Notes: This is the only woodpecker to regularly feed on the ground. Prefers ants and beetles and produces an antacid saliva that neutralizes the acidic defense of ants. Male usually selects nest site, taking up to 12 days to excavate. Can be attracted to your yard with a nest box stuffed with sawdust. Often reuses an old nest. Undulates deeply during flight, flashing reddish orange under its wings and tail and calling "wacka-wacka" loudly.

California Thrasher
Toxostoma redivivum

YEAR-ROUND

Size: 12" (30 cm)

Male: Overall light brown. A rusty wash to lower chest, belly and rump. Long, down-curved dark bill with a white chin and several dark lines that run just below the eyes and across the face. Dark eyes. Long tail.

Female: same as male

Juvenile: similar to adult

Nest: cup; male and female construct; 1–2 broods per year

Eggs: 2–4; pale blue with brown markings

Incubation: 12–14 days; female and male incubate

Fledging: 12–14 days; female and male feed young

Migration: non-migrator

Food: insects, fruit, nuts, small lizards; will come to feeders and birdbaths

Compare: Much larger than Sage Thrasher (p. 311), which has a streaked breast and belly and lacks the long, down-curved bill.

Stan's Notes: Unique to California (endemic). Likes dense brush. Forages on the ground for food, sweeping bill back and forth like a rake to uncover it. Eats seeds under feeders in suburban areas. Often runs with tail cocked up. Often heard before seen. Male sings from perches while female remains hidden. Mimics other birds, repeating phrases and interspersing with low, harsh notes. Female flutters her wings and begs for food in response. Male cares for fledglings while female lays eggs for a second brood. Unable to fly for several days, fledglings follow male around on the ground, learning what to eat.

winter

breeding

Pied-billed Grebe
Podilymbus podiceps

YEAR-ROUND

Size: 12–14" (30–36 cm)

Male: Small and brown with a black chin and fluffy white patch beneath the tail. Black ring around a thick, chicken-like, ivory bill. Winter bill is brown and unmarked.

Female: same as male

Juvenile: paler than adults, with white spots and a gray chest, belly and bill

Nest: floating platform; female and male build; 1 brood per year

Eggs: 5–7; bluish white without markings

Incubation: 22–24 days; female and male incubate

Fledging: 45–60 days; female and male feed the young

Migration: non-migrator in California

Food: crayfish, aquatic insects, fish

Compare: Look for a puffy white patch under the tail and thick, chicken-like bill to help identify.

Stan's Notes: A common resident water bird, often seen diving for food. When disturbed, it slowly sinks like a submarine, quickly compressing its feathers, forcing the air out. Was called Hell-diver due to the length of time it can stay submerged. Able to surface far from where it went under. Well suited to life on water, with short wings, lobed toes, and legs set close to the rear of its body. Swims easily but moves awkwardly on land. Very sensitive to pollution. Builds nest on a floating mat in water. "Grebe" may originate from the Breton word *krib*, meaning "crest," referring to the crested head plumes of many grebes, especially during breeding season.

male
p. 75

female

Bufflehead
Bucephala albeola

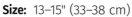

YEAR-ROUND WINTER

Size: 13–15" (33–38 cm)

Female: Brownish-gray duck with a dark brown head. White patch on cheek, just behind the eyes.

Male: striking black-and-white duck with a large bonnet-like white patch on the back of head; head shines greenish-purple in sunlight

Juvenile: similar to female

Nest: cavity; female lines an old woodpecker cavity; 1 brood per year

Eggs: 8–10; ivory-to-olive without markings

Incubation: 29–31 days; female incubates

Fledging: 50–55 days; female leads the young to food

Migration: complete, to California, Mexico and Central America

Food: aquatic insects, crustaceans, mollusks

Compare: The female Lesser Scaup (p. 225) is slightly larger and has a white patch at the base of the bill. Look for the white cheek patch to help identify the female Bufflehead.

Stan's Notes: Common diving duck that travels with other ducks. Usually seen during migrations and winter, arriving late in August. Found on rivers and lakes. Nests in vacant woodpecker holes. When cavities in trees are scarce, known to use a burrow in an earthen bank or will use a nest box. Lines the cavity with fluffy down feathers. Unlike other ducks, the young stay in the nest for up to two days before they venture out with their mothers.

breeding

winter
p. 337

displaying

Willet
Catoptrophorus semipalmatus

SUMMER
MIGRATION
WINTER

Size: 14–16" (36–40 cm)

Male: Brown breeding plumage with a white belly. Brown bill and legs. Distinctive black-and-white wing lining pattern, seen in flight or during display.

Female: same as male

Juvenile: similar to breeding adult, more tan in color

Nest: ground; female builds; 1 brood per year

Eggs: 3–5; olive-green with dark markings

Incubation: 24–28 days; male and female incubate

Fledging: 1–2 days; female and male feed young

Migration: complete, to parts of California, the coast of Mexico, Central and South America

Food: insects, small fish, crabs, worms, clams

Compare: Greater Yellowlegs (p. 211) is slightly smaller and has a smaller head, longer neck and yellow legs. The Marbled Godwit (p. 237) has a two-toned, upturned bill.

Stan's Notes: Common winter resident in California. Northern birds pass through coastal California to destinations farther south. It appears a rich, warm brown during the breeding season and rather plain gray during the winter, but it always has a striking black-and-white wing pattern when seen in flight. Uses its black-and-white wing patches to display to its mate. Named after the "pill-will-willet" call it gives during the breeding season. Gives a "kip-kip-kip" alarm call when it takes flight. It nests in far north-eastern California, other western states, along the East Coast and in Canada.

male
p. 47

female

Great-tailed Grackle
Quiscalus mexicanus

YEAR-ROUND

Size: 15" (38 cm), female
18" (45 cm), male

Female: An overall brown bird with a gray-to-brown belly. Light-brown-to-white eyes, eyebrows, throat and upper portion of chest.

Male: all-black bird with iridescent purple sheen on head and back, exceptionally long tail, bright-yellow eyes

Juvenile: similar to female

Nest: cup; female builds; 1–2 broods per year

Eggs: 3–5; greenish blue with brown markings

Incubation: 12–14 days; female incubates

Fledging: 21–23 days; female feeds young

Migration: non-migrator to partial in California; moves around to find food

Food: insects, fruit, seeds; comes to seed feeders

Compare: Female Brewer's Blackbird (p. 185) is much smaller and has a darker-brown chest. Female Brown-headed Cowbird (p. 169) is much smaller than Great-tailed. Look for Great-tailed Grackle's distinct light-brown eyebrows.

Stan's Notes: This is our largest grackle. It was once considered a subspecies of the Boat-tailed Grackle, which occurs in Florida and along the East and Gulf Coasts. Prefers to nest near water in an open habitat. A colony nester. Males do not participate in nest building, incubation or raising young. Males rarely fight; females squabble over nest sites and materials. Several females mate with one male. They are expanding northward, moving into northern states. Western populations tend to be larger than eastern ones. Song varies from population to population.

Green-winged Teal
Anas crecca

WINTER

Size: 14–15" (36–38 cm)

Male: Chestnut head with a dark-green patch outlined with white from the eyes to the nape of neck. Gray body and butter-yellow tail. Green patch on the wings (speculum), seen in flight.

Female: light-brown duck with black spots and a green speculum, small bill

Juvenile: same as female

Nest: ground; female builds; 1 brood per year

Eggs: 8–10; cream-white without markings

Incubation: 21–23 days; female incubates

Fledging: 32–34 days; female teaches the young to feed

Migration: complete to California

Food: aquatic plants and insects

Compare: The male Green-winged is not as colorful as the male Wood Duck (p. 371). Female Green-winged is very similar to the larger female Cinnamon Teal (p. 223), which lacks the dark line through the eyes and has a larger bill. The female Blue-winged Teal (p. 221) is similar in size and has a slight white mark at base of bill.

Stan's Notes: One of the smallest dabbling ducks. Tips forward in water to feed off the bottom of shallow ponds. This behavior makes it vulnerable to ingesting spent lead shot, which can cause death. It walks well on land and will also feed in flooded fields and woodlands. Known for its fast and agile flight. Groups wheel and spin through the air in tight formation. The green wing patches are most obvious during flight.

Blue-winged Teal
Spatula discors

SUMMER
MIGRATION
WINTER

Size: 15–16" (38–41 cm)

Male: Small, plain-looking brown duck with black speckles and a large, crescent-shaped white mark at the base of the bill. Gray head. Black tail with a small white patch. Blue wing patch (speculum), best seen in flight.

Female: duller than male, with only slight white at the base of the bill; lacks a crescent mark on the face and a white patch on the tail

Juvenile: same as female

Nest: ground; female builds; 1 brood per year

Eggs: 8–11; creamy white

Incubation: 23–27 days; female incubates

Fledging: 35–44 days; female feeds the young

Migration: complete, to California, Mexico and Central America

Food: aquatic plants, seeds, aquatic insects

Compare: The female Mallard (p. 247) has an orange-and-black bill. The female Wood Duck (p. 233) has a crest. Female Green-winged Teal (p. 219) is similar in size but lacks white at base of bill. Look for the white facial mark to identify the male Blue-winged.

Stan's Notes: One of the smallest ducks in North America. Nests some distance from water. Known to hybridize with Cinnamon Teals. Female performs a distraction display to protect nest and young. Male leaves female near the end of incubation. Planting crops and cultivating to pond edges have caused a decline in population. One of the longest distance migrating ducks.

male p. 81

female

Lesser Scaup
Aythya affinis

YEAR-ROUND WINTER

Size: 16–17" (40–43 cm)

Female: Overall brown duck with a dull-white patch at the base of a light-gray bill. Yellow eyes.

Male: white and gray; the chest and head appear nearly black, but the head looks purple with green highlights in direct sun; yellow eyes

Juvenile: same as female

Nest: ground; female builds; 1 brood per year

Eggs: 8–14; olive-buff without markings

Incubation: 22–28 days; female incubates

Fledging: 45–50 days; female teaches young to feed

Migration: complete, to California, Mexico, Central America and northern South America

Food: aquatic plants and insects

Compare: Female Ring-necked Duck (p. 229) is a similar size but has a white ring around the bill. Male Blue-winged Teal (p. 221) is slightly smaller and has a crescent-shaped white mark at base of bill. Female Wood Duck (p. 233) is larger with white around the eyes.

Stan's Notes: A common diving duck. Often seen in large flocks on lakes, ponds and sewage lagoons. Submerges itself completely to feed on the bottom of lakes (unlike dabbling ducks, which only tip forward to reach the bottom). Note the bold white stripe under the wings when in flight. The male leaves the female when she starts incubating eggs. The quantity of eggs (clutch size) increases with the female's age. This species has an interesting babysitting arrangement in which groups of young (crèches) are tended by one to three adult females. A winter resident, it doesn't breed in most of California.

225

soaring

Red-shouldered Hawk
Buteo lineatus

Size: 15–19" (38–48 cm); up to 3½' wingspan

Male: Reddish (cinnamon) head, shoulders, breast and belly. Wings and back are dark brown with white spots. Long tail with thin white bands and wide black bands. Obvious red wing linings, seen in flight.

Female: same as male

Juvenile: similar to adults but lacks the cinnamon color; white chest with dark spots

Nest: platform; female and male build; 1 brood per year

Eggs: 2–4; white with dark markings

Incubation: 27–29 days; female and male incubate

Fledging: 39–45 days; female and male feed the young

Migration: non-migrator to partial migrator; winters in the U.S.

Food: reptiles, amphibians, large insects, birds

Compare: The Red-tailed Hawk (p. 253) has a white chest. Cooper's Hawk (p. 341) has a slimmer body and longer tail. The Sharp-shinned Hawk (p. 339) is smaller and lacks the reddish head and belly of the Red-shouldered Hawk.

Stan's Notes: Common in woodlands and backyards in the state. Likes to hunt at forest edges, spotting snakes, frogs, insects, occasional small birds and other prey as it perches. Often flaps with an alternating gliding pattern. Very vocal with a distinct scream. Breeds when it reaches 2–3 years. Remains in the same territory for many years. Starts constructing its nest in February. Young leave the nest by June.

male p. 83

female

Ring-necked Duck
Aythya collaris

WINTER

Size: 16–19" (41–48 cm)

Female: Brown with a darker-brown back and crown and lighter-brown sides. Gray face. White eye-ring with a white line behind the eye. White ring around the bill. Peaked head.

Male: black head, chest and back; gray-to-white sides; blue bill with a bold white ring and a thinner ring at the base; peaked head

Juvenile: similar to female

Nest: ground; female builds; 1 brood per year

Eggs: 8–10; olive to brown without markings

Incubation: 26–27 days; female incubates

Fledging: 49–56 days; female teaches the young to feed

Migration: complete migrator, to California, Mexico and Central America

Food: aquatic plants and insects

Compare: Female Lesser Scaup (p. 225) is similar in size. Look for the white ring around the bill to help identify the female Ring-necked Duck.

Stan's Notes: A common winter duck throughout the state. Often seen in larger freshwater lakes, usually in small flocks or just pairs. A diving duck, watch for it to dive underwater to forage for food. Springs up off the water to take flight. Has a distinctive tall, peaked head with a sloped forehead. Flattens its crown when diving. Male gives a quick series of grating barks and grunts. Female gives high-pitched peeps. Named "Ring-necked" for its cinnamon collar, which is nearly impossible to see in the field. Also called Ring-billed Duck due to the white ring on its bill.

female

male
p. 85

Hooded Merganser
Lophodytes cucullatus

WINTER

Size: 16–19" (41–48 cm)

Female: Sleek brown-and-rust bird with a red head. Ragged "hair" on the back of the head. Long, thin, brown bill.

Male: black back, rust-brown sides, long black bill; raises crest "hood" to display a white patch

Juvenile: similar to female

Nest: cavity; female lines an old woodpecker cavity or a nest box near water; 1 brood per year

Eggs: 10–12; white without markings

Incubation: 32–33 days; female incubates

Fledging: 71 days; female feeds the young

Migration: complete, to northwestern California

Food: small fish, aquatic insects, crustaceans (especially crayfish)

Compare: Very similar to, but smaller than, the female Red-breasted Merganser (p. 263), which has a larger, lighter colored bill. Female Lesser Scaup (p. 225) is smaller and has a dull-white patch at the base of its bill. Look for the ragged "hair" on the back of the head of the female Hoodie.

Stan's Notes: A small diving duck, found in shallow ponds, sloughs, lakes and rivers. Usually in small groups. Quick, low flight across the water, with fast wingbeats. Male has a deep, rolling call. Female gives a hoarse quack. Nests in wooded areas. Female will lay some eggs in the nests of other mergansers, goldeneyes or Wood Ducks (egg dumping), resulting in 20–25 eggs in some nests. Rarely, she shares a nest, sitting with a Wood Duck.

Marbled Godwit
Limosa fedoa

MIGRATION WINTER

Size: 18" (45 cm)

Male: Tawny brown overall with a darker back. Long, two-toned and slightly upturned bill with black tip and pinkish base. Long gray legs. Cinnamon under wings, seen in flight.

Female: same as male

Juvenile: similar to adult

Nest: ground; female and male construct; 1 brood per year

Eggs: 3–5; olive-green with dark markings

Incubation: 21–23 days; male and female incubate

Fledging: 20–21 days; female and male feed the young

Migration: complete, to coastal California, Mexico and Central America

Food: aquatic insects, snails, worms, leeches

Compare: Breeding Willet (p. 213) is smaller. Whimbrel (p. 235) is the same size and has a down-curved bill, compared with the slightly upturned bill of the Godwit.

Stan's Notes: A winter resident that is easily identified by its very long, two-toned, slightly upturned bill. Uses its bill to probe deep into sand and mud for insects. Usually feeds in mid-thigh water. In the winter, prefers saltwater beaches and mud flats up and down the West Coast. Returns to Prairie Pothole regions of North Dakota and Canada, where it nests in shortgrass prairie near wetlands. Name comes from its "god*whit*-god*whit*" call.

male
p. 89

female

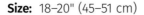

Common Goldeneye
Bucephala clangula

WINTER

Size:	18–20" (45–51 cm)
Female:	Brown-and-gray duck with a large dark-brown head and gray body. White collar. Bright-golden eyes. Yellow-tipped dark bill.
Male:	mostly white with a black back, a puffy green head, a large white spot on the face, bright-golden eyes and a dark bill
Juvenile:	same as female but with a dark bill
Nest:	cavity; female lines an old woodpecker cavity; 1 brood per year
Eggs:	8–10; light green without markings
Incubation:	28–32 days; female incubates
Fledging:	56–59 days; female leads the young to food
Migration:	complete, to California and Mexico
Food:	aquatic plants, insects, fish, mollusks
Compare:	Similar to female Lesser Scaup (p. 225), which is smaller. Look for the dark-brown head, white collar and golden-yellow eye to help identify the female Common Goldeneye. Winter male and female Ruddy Duck (p. 217) are smaller and lack yellow eyes.

Stan's Notes: Known for the loud whistling sound produced by its wings during flight. During late winter and early spring, the male performs elaborate mating displays that include throwing his head back and calling a raspy note. Female will lay some of her eggs in other goldeneye nests or in the nests of other species (egg dumping), causing some mothers to incubate as many as 30 eggs in a brood. Named for its bright-golden eyes. Winters in California where it finds open water.

male
p. 349

female

Gadwall
Mareca strepera

YEAR-ROUND WINTER

Size: 19" (48 cm)

Female: Mottled brown with a pronounced color change from dark-brown body to light-brown neck and head. Bright-white wing linings, seen in flight. Small white wing patch, seen when swimming. Gray bill with orange sides.

Male: plump gray duck with a brown head and distinctive black rump, white belly, bright-white wing linings, small white wing patch, chestnut-tinged wings, gray bill

Juvenile: similar to female

Nest: ground; female lines the nest with fine grass and down feathers plucked from her chest; 1 brood per year

Eggs: 8–11; white without markings

Incubation: 24–27 days; female incubates

Fledging: 48–56 days; young feed themselves

Migration: complete to non-migrator in California

Food: aquatic insects

Compare: Female Mallard (p. 247) is similar but has a blue-and-white wing mark. Look for Gadwall's white wing patch and gray bill with orange sides.

Stan's Notes: A duck of shallow marshes. Consumes mostly plant material, dunking its head in water to feed rather than tipping forward, like other dabbling ducks. Walks well on land; feeds in fields and woodlands. Nests within 300 feet (90 m) of water. Often in pairs with other duck species. Establishes pair bond during winter.

male p. 375

female

Northern Shoveler

Anas clypeata

YEAR-ROUND
WINTER

Size: 19–21" (48–53 cm)

Female: A medium-size brown duck speckled with black. Green patch on the wings (speculum). An extraordinarily large, spoon-shaped bill.

Male: iridescent green head, rusty sides, white chest and a large spoon-shaped bill

Juvenile: same as female

Nest: ground; female builds; 1 brood per year

Eggs: 9–12; olive without markings

Incubation: 22–25 days; female incubates

Fledging: 30–60 days; female leads the young to food

Migration: complete to non-migrator, to California, Mexico, and Central America

Food: aquatic insects, plants

Compare: Female Mallard (p. 247) is similar but lacks the Shoveler's large bill. Female Redhead (p. 243) is overall lighter brown and has a dark-gray bill with a black tip. Look for Shoveler's large spoon-shaped bill to help identify.

Stan's Notes: One of several species of shovelers. Called "Shoveler" due to the peculiar, shovel-like shape of its bill. Given the common name "Northern" because it is the only species of these ducks in North America. Seen in shallow wetlands, ponds and small lakes in flocks of 5–10 birds. Flocks fly in tight formation. Swims low in water, pointing its large bill toward the water as if it's too heavy to lift. Usually swims in tight circles while feeding. Feeds mainly by filtering tiny aquatic insects and plants from the surface of the water with its bill. Winters in California wherever it can find water.

male
p. 373

female

Mallard
Anas platyrhynchos

YEAR-ROUND

Size: 19–21" (48–53 cm)

Female: Brown duck with a blue-and-white wing mark (speculum). Orange-and-black bill.

Male: large green head, white necklace, rust-brown or chestnut chest, gray-and-white sides, yellow bill, orange legs and feet

Juvenile: same as female but with a yellow bill

Nest: ground; female builds; 1 brood per year

Eggs: 7–10; greenish to whitish, unmarked

Incubation: 26–30 days; female incubates

Fledging: 42–52 days; female leads the young to food

Migration: non-migrator to partial in California

Food: seeds, plants, aquatic insects; will come to ground feeders offering corn

Compare: Female Gadwall (p. 241) has a gray bill with orange sides. Female Northern Pintail (p. 249) is similar to female Mallard, but it has a gray bill. Female Northern Shoveler (p. 245) has a spoon-shaped bill. Female Wood Duck (p. 233) has a white eye-ring.

Stan's Notes: A familiar dabbling duck of lakes and ponds. Also found in rivers, streams and some backyards. Tips forward to feed on vegetation on the bottom of shallow water. The name "Mallard" comes from the Latin word *masculus,* meaning "male," referring to the male's habit of taking no part in raising the young. Female and male have white underwings and white tails, but only the male has black central tail feathers that curl upward. The female gives a classic quack. Will return to place of birth.

male
p. 345

female

soaring

Northern Harrier
Circus hudsonius

YEAR-ROUND
WINTER

Size: 18–22" (45–56 cm); up to 4' wingspan

Female: Slender, low-flying hawk with a dark-brown back and brown streaking on the chest and belly. Large white rump patch. Thin black tail bands and black wing tips. Yellow eyes.

Male: silver-gray with a large white rump patch and white belly, black wing tips, yellow eyes, faint, thin bands across the tail

Juvenile: similar to female, with an orange breast

Nest: ground; female and male construct; 1 brood per year

Eggs: 4–8; bluish white without markings

Incubation: 31–32 days; female incubates

Fledging: 30–35 days; male and female feed the young

Migration: non-migrator to partial in California

Food: mice, snakes, insects, small birds

Compare: Slimmer than the Red-tailed Hawk (p. 253). Look for the characteristic low gliding and the black tail bands to identify the female Harrier.

Stan's Notes: One of the easiest of hawks to identify. Glides just above the ground, following the contours of the land while searching for prey. Holds its wings just above horizontal, tilting back and forth in the wind, similar to the Turkey Vulture. Formerly called Marsh Hawk due to its habit of hunting over marshes. Feeds and nests on the ground. Will also preen and rest on the ground. Unlike other hawks, mainly uses its hearing to find prey, followed by its sight. At any age, it has a distinctive owl-like face disk.

soaring

YEAR-ROUND

Red-tailed Hawk
Buteo jamaicensis

Size: 19–23" (48–63 cm); up to 4½' wingspan

Male: Variety of colorations, from chocolate brown to nearly all white. Often brown with a white breast and brown belly band. Rust-red tail. Underside of wing is white with a small dark patch on the leading edge near the shoulder.

Female: same as male but slightly larger

Juvenile: similar to adults, with a speckled breast and light eyes; lacks a red tail

Nest: platform; male and female build; 1 brood per year

Eggs: 2–3; white without markings or sometimes marked with brown

Incubation: 30–35 days; female and male incubate

Fledging: 45–46 days; male and female feed the young

Migration: non-migrator; moves around to find food

Food: small and medium-size animals, large birds, snakes, fish, insects, bats, carrion

Compare: Red-shouldered Hawk (p. 227) is much smaller and lacks a red tail and white chest.

Stan's Notes: Common in open country and cities. Seen perching on fences, freeway lampposts and trees. Look for it circling above open fields and roadsides, searching for prey. Gives a high-pitched scream that trails off. Often builds a large stick nest in large trees along roads. Lines nest with finer material, like evergreen needles. Returns to the same nest site each year. The red tail develops in the second year and is best seen from above.

Great Horned Owl
Bubo virginianus

YEAR-ROUND

Size:	21–25" (53–64 cm); up to 4' wingspan
Male:	Robust brown "horned" owl. Bright-yellow eyes and a V-shaped white throat resembling a necklace. Horizontal barring on the chest.
Female:	same as male but slightly larger
Juvenile:	similar to adults but lacks ear tufts
Nest:	no nest; takes over the nest of a crow, hawk or Great Blue Heron or uses a partial cavity, stump or broken tree; 1 brood per year
Eggs:	2–3; white without markings
Incubation:	26–30 days; female incubates
Fledging:	30–35 days; male and female feed the young
Migration:	non-migrator
Food:	mammals, birds (ducks), snakes, insects
Compare:	Burrowing Owl (p. 191) is much smaller, has long legs and lacks the Great Horned's feather tuft "horns." Over twice the size of its cousin, Western Screech-Owl (p. 315).

Stan's Notes: One of the earliest nesting birds in the state, laying eggs in January and February. Able to hunt in complete darkness due to its excellent hearing. The "horns," or "ears," are tufts of feathers and have nothing to do with hearing. Cannot turn its head all the way around. Wing feathers are ragged on the ends, resulting in silent flight. Eyelids close from the top down, like humans. Fearless, it is one of the few animals that will kill skunks and porcupines. Given that, it is also called the Flying Tiger. Call sounds like "hoo-hoo-hoo-hoooo."

displaying

Greater Roadrunner
Geococcyx californianus

Size: 23" (58 cm)

Male: Overall brown with white streaking. Long, pointed brown bill. Extremely long tail. Blue patch just behind eyes. Short round wings are darker brown than body. Long gray legs with large feet. Has a conspicuous crest that can be raised and lowered.

Female: same as male

Juvenile: similar to adult

Nest: platform, low in a tree, shrub or cactus; the female and male build; 1–2 broods per year

Eggs: 4–6; white without markings

Incubation: 18–20 days; male and female incubate

Fledging: 16–18 days; male and female feed young

Migration: non-migrator

Food: insects, reptiles, small mammals and birds

Compare: This uniquely shaped ground dweller has an extremely long tail, a prominent crest, and is hard to confuse with other birds.

Stan's Notes: Ground dweller with a very long tail and prominent crest when raised. Cuckoo family member known to run quickly across the ground to catch prey. A formidable predator, able to run up to 15 miles (24 km) per hour. Flies short distances, usually in a low glide after a running takeoff. Raises its tail high, lowers it slowly. A slow, descending, low-pitched "coo-coo-coo-coo." Male does most incubating and feeding of young. Performs a distraction display to protect the nest. Young can catch prey four weeks after leaving the nest.

cinnamon
wing linings

Long-billed Curlew
Numenius americanus

SUMMER
MIGRATION
WINTER

Size: 23" (58 cm), including bill

Male: Cinnamon brown with an extremely long, down-curved bill. Long bluish legs. Darker cinnamon wing linings.

Female: same as male, but with a longer bill

Juvenile: same as adults, but with a shorter bill

Nest: ground; female builds; 1 brood per year

Eggs: 5–7; olive-green with brown markings

Incubation: 27–30 days; female and male incubate— the female during day, male at night

Fledging: 32–45 days; female and male feed young

Migration: complete, to parts of California, the coast of Mexico and Central and South America

Food: insects, worms, crabs, eggs

Compare: Spotted Sandpiper (p. 173) is smaller, less than half the size of Long-billed Curlew. Hard to mistake the exceptionally long bill.

Stan's Notes: The largest of shorebirds, with an appropriate name. The extremely long bill is greater than half the length of its body. Female has a longer bill than male. Juvenile has a short bill, which grows into a long bill during the first six months. Uses bill to probe deep into mud for insects and worms. Female incubates during the day, male during the night. Although a shorebird, it is often in grass fields away from the shore. Breeds in open valleys and flatlands. Will fly up to 6 miles (10 km) from nest site to find food. Does not nest in most of California, nesting in other western states such as Utah, Idaho, Wyoming and Montana. Spends the winter along the California coast and Mexico.

winter

breeding

in flight

White-faced Ibis
Plegadis chihi

YEAR-ROUND
SUMMER
MIGRATION

Size: 23" (58 cm); up to 3' wingspan

Male: Appears brown with rusty-red (chestnut) on upper body. Glossy brown with green sheen on lower body. Long, down-curved gray bill. White border on a light red face. Orange-red legs and feet. Deep red eyes. Winter has a gray mask and less chestnut.

Female: same as male

Juvenile: similar to winter adult

Nest: platform, on ground, low in shrub or small tree; female and male build; 1 brood a year

Eggs: 2–4; blue or green with brown markings

Incubation: 21–23 days; female and male incubate

Fledging: 30–35 days; female and male feed young

Migration: complete to non-migrator

Food: insects, crayfish, frogs, small fish, shellfish

Compare: Black Oystercatcher (p. 45) has a red bill and yellow legs. American Avocet (p. 87) is mostly black and white with an upturned bill.

Stan's Notes: Of the three ibis species in the U.S., this is the only one regularly seen in California. Usually found in marshes and estuaries. When near and in good light, appears glossy red with green, blue and purple highlights. Uses its long bill to find and eat aquatic insects and fish. Large groups fly in a straight line. Rapid, shallow wing beat, then a short glide. Nests close to the water in large colonies with egrets and herons. Builds a loose nest of thin twigs, leaves and roots, lined with green leaves. Male spends more time feeding young than the female. Common name comes from the white outline on face.

Ring-necked Pheasant

Phasianus colchicus

YEAR-ROUND

Size:	30–36" (76–91 cm), male, including tail 21–25" (53–64 cm), female, including tail
Male:	Golden-brown body with a long tail. White ring around the neck. Head is purple, green, blue and red.
Female:	smaller and less flamboyant than the male, with brown plumage and a long tail
Juvenile:	similar to female, with a shorter tail
Nest:	ground; female builds; 1 brood per year
Eggs:	8–10; olive brown without markings
Incubation:	23–25 days; female incubates
Fledging:	11–12 days; female leads the young to food
Migration:	non-migrator
Food:	insects, seeds, fruit; visits ground feeders
Compare:	California Quail (p. 323) is much smaller and has a teardrop plume on the forehead. Male Ring-necked is brightly colored.

Stan's Notes: Originally introduced to North America from China in the late 1800s. Common now throughout the U.S. Like many other game birds, its numbers vary greatly, making it common in some years, scarce in others. Seeks shelter during harsh winter weather. To attract females, the male gives a cackling call and then rapidly flutters his wings. Takes off in an explosive flight with fast wingbeats followed by gliding low to the ground. The name "Ring-necked" refers to the white ring around the male's neck. "Pheasant" comes from the Greek word *phaisianos*, which means "bird of the River Phasis" (known today as the Rioni River).

soaring

juvenile

juvenile

Golden Eagle
Aquila chrysaetos

YEAR-ROUND
WINTER

Size: 30–40" (76–102 cm); up to 7¼' wingspan

Male: Uniform dark brown with a golden-yellow head and nape of neck. Yellow around base of bill. Yellow feet.

Female: same as male

Juvenile: similar to adult, with white "wrist" patches and a white base of tail

Nest: platform, on a cliff; female and male build; 1 brood per year

Eggs: 1–2; white with brown markings

Incubation: 43–45 days; female and male incubate

Fledging: 63–75 days; female and male feed young

Migration: non-migrator to partial migrator; moves around to find food in winter

Food: mammals, birds, reptiles, insects

Compare: The Bald Eagle (p. 99) adult is similar, but it has a white head and white tail. Bald Eagle juvenile is often confused with the Golden Eagle juvenile; both are large dark birds with white markings.

Stan's Notes: A large, powerful raptor that has no trouble taking larger prey such as jackrabbits. Hunts by perching or soaring and watching for movement. Inhabits mountainous terrain, requiring large territories to provide a sufficient supply of food. Long-term pair bond, renewing its bond late in winter with spectacular high-flying courtship displays. Usually nests on cliff faces; rarely nests in trees. The well-established nest is used for generations. Will add items to the nest such as antlers, bones and barbed wire.

non-breeding

chick-feeding
adult

breeding

in flight

juvenile

Brown Pelican
Pelecanus occidentalis

YEAR-ROUND
WINTER

Size: 46–50" (117–127 cm); up to 7' wingspan

Male: Brown-gray body with a black belly and an exceptionally long bill. Breeding has a white or yellow head, dark chestnut hind neck and a bright red expandable throat pouch. Non-breeding has a white head and neck and a gray throat pouch.

Female: similar to male

Juvenile: brown with white breast and belly; does not acquire adult plumage until the third year

Nest: ground; female and male build; 1 brood per year

Eggs: 2–4; white without markings

Incubation: 28–30 days; female and male incubate

Fledging: 71–86 days; female and male feed the young

Migration: complete to non-migrator along the coast of California

Food: fish

Compare: Unmistakable bird in California.

Stan's Notes: A coastal bird of California and recently was an endangered species. Suffering from eggshell thinning in the 1970s due to DDT and other pesticides, it is now reestablishing along the East, Gulf and West Coasts. Captures fish by diving headfirst into the ocean, opening its large bill and "netting" fish with its gular pouch. Often seen sitting on posts around marinas. Nests in large colonies. Doesn't breed before the age of 3, when it obtains its breeding plumage. The Pacific variety (shown) has a bright-red throat pouch unlike the brown patch of the Atlantic and Gulf Coast birds.

Ruby-crowned Kinglet
Regulus calendula

SUMMER
WINTER

Size:	4" (10 cm)
Male:	Small, teardrop-shaped green-to-gray bird. Two white wing bars and a white eye-ring. Hidden ruby crown.
Female:	same as male, but lacks a ruby crown
Juvenile:	same as female
Nest:	pendulous; female builds; 1 brood per year
Eggs:	4–5; white with brown markings
Incubation:	11–12 days; female incubates
Fledging:	11–12 days; female and male feed the young
Migration:	complete, to California, Mexico
Food:	insects, berries
Compare:	The female American Goldfinch (p. 423) shares the drab olive plumage and unmarked chest, but it is larger. Look for the white eye-ring to identify the Ruby-crowned Kinglet.

Stan's Notes: This is one of the smaller birds in the state. Most commonly seen during the spring and autumn migrations. Look for it flitting around thick shrubs low to the ground. It takes a quick eye to see the ruby crown, which the male flashes when he is excited. The female weaves an unusually intricate nest and fastens colorful lichens and mosses to the exterior with spiderwebs. Often builds the nest high in a mature tree, where it hangs from a branch that has overlapping leaves. Sings a distinctive song that starts out soft and ends loud and on a higher note. "Kinglet" originates from the word *king,* referring to the male's red crown, and the diminutive suffix *let,* meaning "small." A winter resident in most of California.

Bushtit

Psaltriparus minimus

YEAR-ROUND

Size: 4½" (11 cm)

Male: Dull gray with a slightly brown cap. Relatively long tail. Black eyes and legs. Tiny black bill.

Female: same as male, but has pale-yellow eyes

Juvenile: similar to adults, with dark-brown eyes

Nest: pendulous; female and male construct; 1–2 broods per year

Eggs: 5–7; white without markings

Incubation: 10–12 days; female and male incubate

Fledging: 14–15 days; female and male feed young

Migration: non-migrator

Food: insects, seeds, fruit; comes to seed feeders

Compare: Chestnut-backed (p. 123) and Mountain (p. 289) Chickadees are larger and have black crowns and white on their faces. Oak Titmouse (p. 293) has a crest.

Stan's Notes: A lively bird, often seen in extended family flocks of up to 20 individuals in open woods and low woodlands. Often seen with other species of birds, such as kinglets, wrens and chickadees. Easily picked out by its small size, long tail and the extremely short bill. Groups will roost together, huddling tightly to keep warm and save energy. Eyes are pale yellow in adult females, dark brown in juveniles and black in adult males.

male
juvenile
female

YEAR-ROUND

Verdin
Auriparus flaviceps

Size: 4½" (11 cm)

Male: Light gray to silvery overall. Lemon-yellow head. Rusty-red shoulder patch, frequently hidden. Short, pointed dark bill. Dark mark between bill and eyes. Dark legs and feet.

Female: duller than male

Juvenile: overall gray, lacks the yellow head, dark bill and rusty-red shoulder patch

Nest: covered cup; male builds; 1–2 broods a year

Eggs: 4–5; bluish green with brown markings

Incubation: 8–10 days; female incubates

Fledging: 19–21 days; female and male feed young

Migration: non-migrator

Food: seeds, insects, fruit, nectar; comes to nectar feeders and orange halves

Compare: Smaller than the Oak Titmouse (p. 293), which has a crest and lacks a yellow head. Mountain Chickadee (p. 289) has an obvious black cap, chin and eye line.

Stan's Notes: A very friendly bird that can be a regular visitor to nectar feeders and orange halves. Often hides its rusty-red shoulder marks, confusing the novice bird watcher. Most easily identified as a tiny gray bird with a yellow head. Male builds several ball-shaped, conspicuous nests of thorny twigs, interweaves them with leaves and grass and lines them with feathers and plant down. Male shows the nest possibilities to female and she selects one. After fledging, young return to nest at night, unlike most small birds, which leave and don't return for shelter. Often uses nest for several seasons.

Red-breasted Nuthatch
Sitta canadensis

YEAR-ROUND
WINTER

Size: 4½" (11 cm)

Male: Gray-backed bird with an obvious black eye line and black cap. Rust-red breast and belly.

Female: duller than male and has a gray cap and pale undersides

Juvenile: same as female

Nest: cavity; male and female excavate a cavity or move into a vacant hole; 1 brood per year

Eggs: 5–6; white with red-brown markings

Incubation: 11–12 days; female incubates

Fledging: 14–20 days; female and male feed the young

Migration: non-migrator to irruptive; moves around in winter in search of food

Food: insects, insect eggs, seeds; comes to seed and suet feeders

Compare: Pygmy Nuthatch (p. 275) is smaller and White-breasted Nuthatch (p. 285) is larger, and neither has the rust-red breast and black eye line of Red-breasted Nuthatch.

Stan's Notes: The nuthatch climbs down trunks of trees headfirst, searching for insects. Like a chickadee, it grabs a seed from a feeder and flies off to crack it open. It wedges the seed into a crevice and pounds it open with several sharp blows. The name "Nuthatch" comes from the Middle English moniker *nuthak,* referring to the habit of hacking seeds open. Look for it in mature conifers, where it extracts seeds from pine cones. Excavates a cavity or takes an old woodpecker hole or a natural cavity and builds a nest within. Gives a series of nasal "yank-yank-yank" calls.

White-breasted Nuthatch
Sitta carolinensis

YEAR-ROUND

Size: 5–6" (13–15 cm)

Male: Slate gray with a white face, breast and belly. Large white patch on the rump. Black cap and nape. Bill is long and thin, slightly upturned. Chestnut undertail.

Female: similar to male, but has a gray cap and nape

Juvenile: similar to female

Nest: cavity; female and male build a nest within; 1 brood per year

Eggs: 5–7; white with brown markings

Incubation: 11–12 days; female incubates

Fledging: 13–14 days; female and male feed the young

Migration: non-migrator

Food: insects, insect eggs, seeds; comes to seed and suet feeders

Compare: Red-breasted Nuthatch (p. 283) is smaller and has a rust-red belly and distinctive black eye line. Pygmy Nuthatch (p. 275) is smaller and lacks White-breasted's black cap.

Stan's Notes: The nuthatch hops headfirst down trees, looking for insects missed by birds climbing up. Its climbing agility is due to an extra-long hind toe claw, or nail, that is nearly twice the size of its front claws. "Nuthatch," from the Middle English *nuthak,* refers to the bird's habit of wedging a seed in a crevice and hacking it open. Often seen in flocks with Brown Creepers, chickadees and Downy Woodpeckers. Mates stay together year-round, defending a small territory. Gives a characteristic "whi-whi-whi-whi" spring call during February and March. One of nearly 30 worldwide nuthatch species.

YEAR-ROUND

Mountain Chickadee
Poecile gambeli

Size: 5½" (14 cm)

Male: Gray overall with a black cap, chin and line through the eyes. White eyebrows.

Female: same as male

Juvenile: similar to adult

Nest: cavity, old woodpecker hole or excavates its own; female and male build; 1–2 broods per year

Eggs: 5–8; white without markings

Incubation: 11–14 days; female and male incubate

Fledging: 18–21 days; female and male feed the young

Migration: non-migrator to partial migrator

Food: seeds, insects; visits seed and suet feeders

Compare: Larger than Bushtit (p. 277), which lacks the black cap and white on the face. Oak Titmouse (p. 293) is larger and has a crest. Verdin (p. 281) is smaller and has a yellow head.

Stan's Notes: An abundant bird in the state, but most common in coniferous forests in mountainous regions of California. Prefers old-growth spruce, fir and pine forests. Feeds heavily on coniferous seeds and insects. Flocks with other birds during winter. Moves to lower elevations in winter, returning to high elevations for nesting. Excavates a nest cavity or uses an old woodpecker hole. Will use a nest box. Occasionally uses the same nest site year after year. Lines its nest with moss, hair and feathers. Female will not leave her nest if disturbed, but will hiss and flutter wings.

female
p. 137

male

Oregon
male

Dark-eyed Junco
Junco hyemalis

YEAR-ROUND
WINTER

Size: 5½" (14 cm)

Male: Plump, dark-eyed bird with a slate-gray-to-charcoal chest, head and back. White belly. Pink bill. White outer tail feathers appear like a white V in flight.

Female: round with brown plumage

Juvenile: similar to female, with streaking on the breast and head

Nest: cup; female and male build; 2 broods per year

Eggs: 3–5; white with reddish-brown markings

Incubation: 12–13 days; female incubates

Fledging: 10–13 days; male and female feed the young

Migration: partial to non-migrator in California

Food: seeds, insects; visits ground and seed feeders

Compare: Rarely confused with any other bird. Look for small flocks under feeders in winter.

Stan's Notes: One of the most numerous wintering birds in the state. A common year-round resident in parts of California. Spends winters in foothills and plains, returning to higher elevations for nesting. Females tend to migrate farther south than males. Adheres to a rigid social hierarchy, with dominant birds chasing the less dominant birds. Look for the white outer tail feathers flashing in flight. Often seen in small flocks on the ground, where it uses its feet to simultaneously "double-scratch" to expose seeds and insects. Eats many weed seeds. Nests in a wide variety of wooded habitats in April and May. Several sub-species of Dark-eyed Junco were previously considered to be separate species (see lower inset).

female

male p. 393

Vermilion Flycatcher
Pyrocephalus rubinus

YEAR-ROUND
SUMMER
WINTER

Size: 6" (15 cm)

Female: A mostly gray bird with a gray head, neck and back. Nearly white chin and chest. Pink belly to undertail. Black tail. Thin black bill.

Male: crimson-red head, crest, chin, breast and belly, black nape of neck, back, wings and tail, black line through eyes, thin black bill

Juvenile: similar to female, lacks a pink undertail

Nest: cup; female builds; 1–2 broods per year

Eggs: 2–4; white with brown markings

Incubation: 14–16 days; female and male incubate

Fledging: 14–16 days; female and male feed young

Migration: partial migrator to non-migrator in parts of southern California

Food: insects (mainly bees)

Compare: Black Phoebe and Say's Phoebe (pp. 59 and 303) have similar body and bill shapes and share a similar habitat. Black Phoebe is black with a white belly. Say's Phoebe has a pale-orange belly.

Stan's Notes: Frequently seen in open areas with shrubs and small trees close to water. Will perch on a thin branch, pumping tail up and down while waiting for an aerial insect. Flies out to snatch it, then returns to perch. Drops to the ground for terrestrial insects. Male raises its crest, fluffs chest feathers, fans tail and sings a song during a fluttery flight to court females. Female builds a shallow nest of twigs and grasses and lines it with downy plant material. Male feeds female during incubation and brooding.

breeding
p. 151

winter

Least Sandpiper

Calidris minutilla

MIGRATION
WINTER

Size: 6" (15 cm)

Male: Winter plumage is overall gray to light brown, with a distinct brown breast band and white belly. Light-gray eyebrows and short, thin, down-curved black bill. Dull-yellow legs.

Female: same as male

Juvenile: similar to winter adult, but buff-brown and lacks the breast band

Nest: ground; male and female construct; 1 brood per year

Eggs: 3–4; olive with dark markings

Incubation: 19–23 days; male and female incubate

Fledging: 25–28 days; male and female feed the young

Migration: complete, to parts of California, Mexico and Central America

Food: aquatic and terrestrial insects, seeds

Compare: The smallest of sandpipers. Often confused with winter Western Sandpiper (p. 301). Least Sandpiper's yellow legs differentiate it from other tiny sandpipers. Look for the short, thin, down-curved bill to help identify.

Stan's Notes: A winter resident in parts of California. This is a tiny, tame sandpiper that can be approached without scaring. It is the smallest of peeps (sandpipers), nesting on the tundra in northern regions of Canada and Alaska. Prefers the grassy flats of saltwater and freshwater ponds. Its yellow legs can be hard to see in water, poor light or when covered with mud. Most other small shorebirds have black legs and feet.

breeding
p. 153

winter

Western Sandpiper
Calidris mauri

MIGRATION
WINTER

Size: 6½" (16 cm)

Male: Winter plumage is dull gray to light brown overall with a white belly and eyebrows. Black legs. Narrow bill that droops near tip.

Female: same as male

Juvenile: similar to breeding adult, bright buff-brown on the back only

Nest: ground; male and female construct; 1 brood per year

Eggs: 2–4; light brown with dark markings

Incubation: 20–22 days; male and female incubate

Fledging: 19–21 days; male and female feed the young

Migration: complete, to coastal California, Mexico and Central America

Food: aquatic and terrestrial insects

Compare: Winter Least Sandpiper (p. 299) is similar but lacks black legs. Look for black legs and a longer bill that droops slightly at the tip to identify the Western Sandpiper.

Stan's Notes: A winter resident along coastal California and long-distance migrant. Nests on the ground in large "loose" colonies on the tundra of northern coastal Alaska. Adults leave their breeding grounds several weeks before the young. Some obtain their breeding plumage before leaving Florida in spring. Feeds on insects at the water's edge, sometimes immersing its head. Young leave the nest (precocial) within a few hours after hatching. Female leaves and the male tends the hatchlings.

Say's Phoebe
Sayornis saya

YEAR-ROUND
SUMMER
MIGRATION
WINTER

Size: 7½" (19 cm)

Male: Overall dark gray, darkest on head, tail and wings. Belly and undertail tawny. Black bill.

Female: same as male

Juvenile: similar to adult, but browner overall with 2 tawny wing bars and a yellow lower bill

Nest: cup; female builds; 1–2 broods per year

Eggs: 3–6; pale white with brown markings

Incubation: 12–14 days; female incubates

Fledging: 14–16 days; female and male feed young

Migration: partial to non-migrator, to coastal and southern California, Mexico and Central and South America

Food: insects, berries

Compare: Female Vermilion Flycatcher (p. 297) is smaller and has a pink belly.

Stan's Notes: Widespread throughout California below 9,000-foot (2,750 m) elevations. Nests in cliff crevices, abandoned buildings, bridges and other vertical structures. Frequently uses the same nest a couple of times in a season, returning the following year to that same nest. Has a nearly all-insect diet. Flies out from a perch to grab an aerial insect and returns to the same perch (hawking). Also hunts insects on the ground, hovering and dropping down to catch them. Phoebes are classified as New World Flycatchers and aren't related to Old World Flycatchers. Named after Thomas Say, who is said to have first recorded this bird in Colorado. The genus, species and first part of its common name refer to Mr. Say. Common name "Phoebe" is likely an imitation of the bird's call.

YEAR-ROUND

American Dipper
Cinclus mexicanus

Size: 7½" (19 cm)

Male: Dark gray to black overall. Head is slightly lighter in color. Short upturned tail. Dark eyes and bill.

Female: same as male

Juvenile: similar to adult, only paler with white eyelids that are most noticeable when blinking

Nest: pendulous, covered nest with the entrance near the bottom; on cliffs, behind waterfalls; female builds; 1–2 broods per year

Eggs: 3–5; white without markings

Incubation: 13–17 days; female incubates

Fledging: 18–25 days; female and male feed young

Migration: non-migrator; seeks moving open water

Food: aquatic insects, small fish, crustaceans

Compare: American Robin (p. 319) is a similar shape, but it has a red breast. The Dipper is the only songbird in the state that dives into fast-moving water.

Stan's Notes: A bird of fast, usually noisy streams that provide some kind of protected shelf on which to construct a nest. Some birders have had success attracting dippers with man-made ledges. Plunges headfirst into fast-moving water, looking for just about any aquatic insect, propelling itself underwater with its wings. Frequently seen emerging with a large insect, which it smashes against rock before eating. Has the ability to fly directly into the air from underwater. Depending on snowmelt, nesting usually starts in March or April. American Dippers in lower elevations often nest for a second time each season.

breeding
p. 175

winter

Sanderling
Calidris alba

Size: 8" (20 cm)

Male: The lightest sandpiper on the beach during winter. Winter plumage has gray head and back and white belly. Black legs and bill. White wing stripe, seen only in flight.

Female: same as male

Juvenile: spotty black on the head and back with a white belly; black legs and bill

Nest: ground; male builds; 1–2 broods per year

Eggs: 3–4; greenish olive with brown markings

Incubation: 24–30 days; male and female incubate

Fledging: 16–17 days; female and male feed the young

Migration: complete, to coastal California, Mexico, Central and South America

Food: insects

Compare: Breeding Spotted Sandpiper (p. 173) is the same size, but it has black spots on the breast and belly. Winter Spotted is similar but has a light-colored bill and yellow legs. Winter Black-bellied Plover (p. 327) has a similar color but is much larger with a larger bill.

Stan's Notes: One of the most common shorebirds in the state, but seen in gray winter plumage from August to April. Seen in groups on sandy beaches, running out with each retreating wave to feed. Look for a flash of white on the wings when it is in flight. Both sexes perform a distraction display if threatened. Rests by standing on one leg and tucking the other into its belly feathers. Often hops away on one leg, moving away from pedestrians on the beach. Surveys show a large decline in numbers since the 1970s.

Sage Thrasher
Oreoscoptes montanus

SUMMER
MIGRATION
WINTER

Size: 8½" (22 cm)

Male: Light gray overall with a heavily streaked white chest. Distinctive white chin. Yellow-orange eyes. Darker gray tail with white tip.

Female: same as male

Juvenile: duller version of adult

Nest: cup; the female and male build; 1–2 broods per year

Eggs: 3–5; blue with brown markings

Incubation: 13–17 days; female and male incubate

Fledging: 11–14 days; female and male feed young

Migration: complete, to southern California, Mexico and Central America

Food: insects, fruit

Compare: The California Thrasher (p. 201) is much larger and lacks a streaked breast and belly. Cactus Wren (p. 179) has bold white eyebrows and a down-curved bill. Northern Mockingbird (p. 321) has white wing patches, as seen in flight.

Stan's Notes: More common in the sagebrush regions, which are known for unique birdlife. Males are often seen and heard as they sing from the tops of shrubs. Will construct a large and bulky nest at the base of or beneath dense cover in an attempt to keep the nest shaded. Sometimes constructs a twig platform over nest if existing cover doesn't provide enough shade. Old nests are sometimes used by Gambel's Quails. Returns in to nesting grounds in April and nests in May. Populations increasing in California over the past few decades.

Townsend's Solitaire

Myadestes townsendi

YEAR-ROUND
WINTER

Size: 8½" (22 cm)

Male: All-gray robin look-alike. Prominent white ring around each eye. Wings slightly darker than the body. Long tail. Short dark bill. Dark legs.

Female: same as male

Juvenile: darker gray with a tan, scaly appearance

Nest: cup; female builds; 1–2 broods per year

Eggs: 3–5; blue, green, gray or white with brown markings

Incubation: 12–14 days; female incubates

Fledging: 10–14 days; female and male feed young

Migration: non-migrator to partial in parts of California; known to migrate to eastern states

Food: insects, fruit

Compare: American Robin (p. 319) has a red breast. The Northern Mockingbird (p. 321) lacks the white eye-ring. Clark's Nutcracker (p. 329) has black wings.

Stan's Notes: A summer resident of coniferous mountain forests, moving lower in winter. "Hawks" for insects, perching in trees and darting out to capture them. Eats berries in winter when insects are not available and actively defends a good berry source from other birds. Builds nest on ground sheltered by rocks or an overhang, or sometimes low in a tree or shrub. Song is a series of clear flute-like whistles without a distinct pattern. Shows white outer tail feathers and light-tan patches on wings when in flight.

Loggerhead Shrike
Lanius ludovicianus

YEAR-ROUND
MIGRATION

Size: 9" (22.5 cm)

Male: Gray head and back and a white chin, breast and belly. Black wings, tail, legs and feet. Black mask across the eyes and a black bill with a hooked tip. White wing patches, seen in flight.

Female: same as male

Juvenile: dull version of adult

Nest: cup; male and female construct; 1–2 broods per year

Eggs: 4–7; off-white with dark markings

Incubation: 16–17 days; female incubates

Fledging: 17–21 days; female and male feed the young

Migration: non-migrator to partial in California; moves around to find food in winter

Food: insects, lizards, small mammals, frogs

Compare: The Northern Mockingbird (p. 321) has a similar color pattern, but it lacks the black mask. The Cedar Waxwing (p. 171) has a black mask, but it is a brown bird, not gray and black like the Loggerhead Shrike.

Stan's Notes: The Loggerhead is a songbird that acts like a bird of prey. Known for skewering prey on barbed wire fences, thorns and other sharp objects to store or hold still while tearing apart to eat, hence its other common name, Butcher Bird. Feet are too weak to hold the prey it eats. Breeding bird surveys indicate declining populations in many places due to pesticides killing its major food source—grasshoppers.

American Robin
Turdus migratorius

**YEAR-ROUND
WINTER**

Size: 9–11" (23–28 cm)

Male: Familiar gray bird with a dark rust-red breast and a nearly black head and tail. White chin with black streaks. White eye-ring.

Female: similar to male, with a duller rust-red breast and a gray head

Juvenile: similar to female, with a speckled breast and brown back

Nest: cup; female builds with help from the male; 2–3 broods per year

Eggs: 4–7; pale blue without markings

Incubation: 12–14 days; female incubates

Fledging: 14–16 days; female and male feed the young

Migration: non-migrator to partial in California

Food: insects, fruit, berries, earthworms

Compare: Familiar bird to all. To differentiate the male from the female, compare the nearly black head and rust-red chest of the male with the gray head and duller chest of the female.

Stan's Notes: Although sometimes a complete migrator in northern states, it is a year-round resident in much of California. Can be heard singing all night long in spring. City robins sing louder than country robins in order to hear one another over traffic and noise. A robin isn't listening for worms when it turns its head to one side. It is focusing its sight out of one eye to look for dirt moving, which is caused by worms moving. Territorial, often fighting its reflection in a window. Northern birds join resident birds in California during winter, increasing the population.

YEAR-ROUND

California Quail
Callipepla californica

Size: 10" (25 cm)

Male: Plump gray quail with black face and chin. Prominent teardrop-shaped plume on the forehead. "Scaled" appearance on the belly, light brown to white. Pale-brown forehead.

Female: similar to male, lacks a black face and chin

Juvenile: similar to female

Nest: ground; female builds; 1 brood per year

Eggs: 12–16; white with brown markings

Incubation: 18–23 days; female incubates

Fledging: 8–10 days; female and male teach young to feed

Migration: non-migrator

Food: seeds, leaves, insects; visits ground feeders

Compare: Male Gambel's Quail (p. 325) is the same size with a rusty-red crest and dark patch on the belly. Ring-necked Pheasant (p. 265) is larger and lacks the unique plume on the head of the Quail.

Stan's Notes: Prefers open fields, agricultural areas and sagebrush. Not found in dense forests or at high elevations. Rarely flies, preferring to run away. Roosts in trees or dense shrubs at night, not on the ground. Usually seen in groups (coveys) of up to 100 individuals during winter, breaking up into small family units for breeding. Young stay with the family group until autumn. Has expanded its range in California over the past 60 years.

male

female

Gambel's Quail
Callipepla gambelii

YEAR-ROUND

Size: 10" (25 cm)

Male: A plump, round bird with a short tail. Gray chest, back and tail. Rusty crest outlined in white. Dark chin, throat and forehead with a unique dark plume emanating from the forehead. Rusty sides with white streaks. A dark patch on belly. Black bill. Gray legs.

Female: similar to male, lacks a rusty crest and dark chin, throat and forehead; plume less robust

Juvenile: similar to female

Nest: ground; female builds; 1–2 broods per year

Eggs: 8–12; dull white with brown markings

Incubation: 21–24 days; female incubates

Fledging: 7–10 days; female and male show the young what to eat

Migration: non-migrator

Food: seeds, leaves, insects, fruit; comes to seed feeders on the ground

Compare: California Quail (p. 323) lacks the male's dark belly patch and rusty-red crest.

Stan's Notes: A native species. Prefers arid scrubby regions with a constant water source. Winter flocks of up to 20 birds (coveys) split up during breeding season. Covey walks in single file. Able to hop on and over fences. Scurries across open areas to reach cover. Visits feeders in early morning and late afternoon. Takes dust baths in dirt depressions, kicking dust over body to get rid of small insects. Builds cup nest under vegetation, lining it with grass and feathers. Male gives a distinctive, repeating call, "yup-waay-yup-yup."

Eurasian Collared-Dove
Streptopelia decaocto

YEAR-ROUND

Size: 12½" (32 cm)

Male: Head, neck, breast and belly are gray to tan. Back, wings and tail are slightly darker. Thin black collar with a white border on the nape of the neck. Tail is long and squared.

Female: same as male

Juvenile: similar to adults

Nest: platform; female and male build; 2–3 broods per year

Eggs: 3–5; creamy white without markings

Incubation: 12–14 days; female and male incubate

Fledging: 12–14 days; female and male feed the young

Migration: non-migrator

Food: seeds; will visit ground and seed feeders

Compare: The Mourning Dove (p. 203) is slightly smaller and darker. The Rock Pigeon (p. 333) has colorful iridescent patches. Look for the black collar on the nape and the squared tail to help identify the Eurasian Collared-Dove.

Stan's Notes: This non-native bird has spread into California, having moved into Florida in the early 1980s after inadvertent introduction to the Bahamas. It has been expanding its range across North America and is predicted to spread just like it did through Europe from Asia. Unknown how this "new" bird will affect populations of the native Mourning Dove. Nearly identical to the Ringed Turtle-Dove, a common pet bird. The dark mark on the back of the neck gave rise to the common name. Look for flashes of white in the tail and dark wing tips when it lands or takes off.

YEAR-ROUND

Rock Pigeon
Columba livia

Size: 13" (33 cm)

Male: No set color pattern. Shades of gray to white with patches of gleaming, iridescent green and blue. Often has a light rump patch.

Female: same as male

Juvenile: same as adults

Nest: platform; female builds; 3–4 broods per year

Eggs: 1–2; white without markings

Incubation: 18–20 days; female and male incubate

Fledging: 25–26 days; female and male feed the young

Migration: non-migrator

Food: seeds

Compare: The larger Band-tailed Pigeon (p. 335) is uniformly colored and patterned and has a disproportionately long tail. The Eurasian Collared-Dove (p. 331) has a black collar on the nape. The Mourning Dove (p. 203) is smaller and light brown and lacks the variety of color combinations of the Rock Pigeon.

Stan's Notes: Also known as the Domestic Pigeon. Formerly known as the Rock Dove. Introduced to North America from Europe by the early settlers. One of the few birds with a wide variety of colors, produced by years of selective breeding while in captivity. Parents feed the young a regurgitated liquid known as crop-milk for the first few days of life. One of the few birds that can drink without tilting its head back. Nests under bridges or on buildings, balconies, barns and sheds. Was once thought to be a nuisance in cities and was poisoned. Now, many cities have Peregrine Falcons (p. 343) feeding on Rock Pigeons, which keeps their numbers in check.

YEAR-ROUND

Band-tailed Pigeon
Patagioenas fasciata

Size: 14½" (37 cm)

Male: A typical pigeon-shaped body. Overall gray with a narrow white band on nape of neck. Dark eyes. Black-tipped yellow bill. Yellow legs. Disproportionately long tail.

Female: same as male

Juvenile: similar to adult, lacks white band on neck

Nest: cup; female and male construct; 2–3 broods per year

Eggs: 1–2; white without markings

Incubation: 18–20 days; female and male incubate

Fledging: 25–27 days; female and male feed young

Migration: non-migrator

Food: nuts, seeds, fruit, berries

Compare: The smaller Rock Pigeon (p. 333) comes in a wide variety of colors and patterns, unlike the uniformly colored and patterned Band-tailed. Look for a long tail and the uniform color of Band-taileds in a flock.

Stan's Notes: A common pigeon in mountainous parts of the state. Prefers residential areas and city parks with suitable large conifer trees, in low to middle elevations. Has a nomadic lifestyle. Moves around constantly in response to the food supply. Often seen flying in groups. Male performs a courtship flight of rapid flapping alternating with short glides, then landing and bowing to female. Nests in scattered pairs. Easily distinguished from the Rock Pigeon by its uniform gray color and long tail.

soaring

juvenile

Sharp-shinned Hawk
Accipiter striatus

YEAR-ROUND
WINTER

Size: 10–14" (25–36 cm); up to 2' wingspan

Male: Small woodland hawk with a gray back and head and a rust-red chest. Short wings. Long, squared tail and several dark tail bands, with the widest at the end of the tail. Red eyes.

Female: same as male but larger

Juvenile: same size as adults, with a brown back, heavy streaking on the chest and yellow eyes

Nest: platform; female builds; 1 brood per year

Eggs: 4–5; white with brown markings

Incubation: 32–35 days; female incubates

Fledging: 24–27 days; female and male feed the young

Migration: complete to non-migrator in California

Food: birds, small mammals

Compare: Cooper's Hawk (p. 341) is larger and has a larger head, a slightly longer neck and a rounded tail. The Red-shouldered Hawk (p. 227) has a reddish head and belly.

Stan's Notes: A common hawk of backyards, parks and woodlands. Seen swooping on birds visiting feeders and chasing them as they flee. Its short wingspan and long tail help it to maneuver through thick stands of trees in pursuit of prey. Calls a loud, high-pitched "kik-kik-kik-kik." Named "Sharp-shinned" for the sharp projection (keel) on the leading edge of its shin. A bird's shin is actually below the ankle (rather than above it, like ours) on the tarsus bone of its foot. In most birds, the tarsus bone is rounded, not sharp.

juvenile

in-flight juvenile

in flight

Peregrine Falcon
Falco peregrinus

YEAR-ROUND
WINTER

Size: 16–20" (41–51 cm); up to 3¾' wingspan

Male: Dark-gray back and tan-to-white chest. Horizontal bars on belly, legs and undertail. Dark "hood" head marking and wide black mustache. Yellow base of bill and eye-ring. Yellow legs.

Female: similar to male but noticeably larger

Juvenile: overall darker than adults, with heavy streaking on the chest and belly

Nest: ground (scrape) on a cliff edge, tall building, bridge or smokestack; 1 brood per year

Eggs: 3–4; white, some with brown markings

Incubation: 29–32 days; female and male incubate

Fledging: 35–42 days; male and female feed the young

Migration: partial to non-migrator; moves around to find food

Food: birds (Rock Pigeons in cities, shorebirds and waterfowl in rural areas)

Compare: The American Kestrel (p. 193) is smaller and has 2 vertical black stripes on its face. Look for the dark "hood" head marking and mustache marks to identify the Peregrine Falcon.

Stan's Notes: A wide-bodied raptor that hunts many bird species. The larger females hunt larger prey. Lives in many cities, diving (stooping) on pigeons at speeds of up to 200 miles (322 km) per hour, which knocks them to the ground. Soars with its wings flat, often riding thermals. During courtship, the male brings food to the female and performs aerial displays. Likes to nest on a high ledge or platform for a good view of its territory. A solitary nester and monogamous.

343

female
p. 251

male

soaring

Northern Harrier
Circus hudsonius

YEAR-ROUND WINTER

Size: 18–22" (45–56 cm); up to 4' wingspan

Male: Slender, low-flying hawk. Silver-gray with a large white rump patch and white belly. Long tail with faint narrow bands. Black wing tips. Yellow eyes.

Female: dark-brown back, brown streaking on breast and belly, large white rump patch, thin black tail bands, black wing tips, yellow eyes

Juvenile: similar to female, with an orange breast

Nest: ground; female and male construct; 1 brood per year

Eggs: 4–8; bluish white without markings

Incubation: 31–32 days; female incubates

Fledging: 30–35 days; male and female feed the young

Migration: non-migrator to partial in California

Food: mice, snakes, insects, small birds

Compare: Slimmer than the Red-tailed Hawk (p. 253). Cooper's Hawk (p. 341) has a rusty breast. Look for a low-gliding hawk with a large white rump patch to identify the male Harrier.

Stan's Notes: One of the easiest of hawks to identify. Glides just above the ground, following the contours of the land while searching for prey. Holds its wings just above horizontal, tilting back and forth in the wind, similar to Turkey Vultures. Formerly called the Marsh Hawk due to its habit of hunting over marshes. Feeds and nests on the ground. Will also preen and rest on the ground. Unlike other hawks, mainly uses its hearing to find prey, followed by sight. At any age, has a distinctive owl-like face disk.

breeding

in flight
breeding

juvenile

winter

in flight
juvenile

Heermann's Gull

Larus heermanni

MIGRATION
WINTER

Size: 19" (48 cm); up to 4½' wingspan

Male: An overall dark gray gull with a white head. Distinctive darker wings and tail, both with white edges, as seen in flight. Black-tipped orange bill. Winter lacks a white head.

Female: same as male

Juvenile: light brown with a dark head and a black-tipped yellow bill

Nest: ground; female and male construct; 1 brood per year

Eggs: 2–3; dull white with brown markings

Incubation: 24–28 days; female and male incubate

Fledging: 28–30 days; female and male feed young

Migration: complete, to coastal California and Mexico, Central America

Food: fish, aquatic insects

Compare: California Gull (p. 403) and Western Gull (p. 405) are both larger and mostly white. Heermann's is the darkest gull on the beach.

Stan's Notes: One of the easiest gulls to identify due to its dark color. An unusual migratory dispersal with many moving up from Mexico, where they nest, to winter on the California coast. Nest is a shallow depression or scrape. Some are sparsely lined. Some nest in tall grass, smashing down plants to create a cup. Nest is usually on isolated islands or coastal flats. Juveniles are light brown through the first winter. Second-year birds are dark gray to brown. Achieves breeding plumage in third year. Fewer than 1 in 250 breeding birds have a conspicuous white patch on their wings, as seen in flight.

male

female
p. 241

Gadwall
Mareca strepera

Size: 20" (48 cm)

Male: A plump gray duck with a brown head and a distinctive black rump. White belly. Chestnut-tinged wings. Bright-white wing linings. Small white wing patch, seen when swimming. Gray bill.

Female: similar to female Mallard, a mottled brown with a pronounced color change from dark-brown body to light-brown neck and head, bright-white wing linings, small white wing patch, gray bill with orange sides

Juvenile: similar to female

Nest: ground; female lines the nest with fine grass and down feathers plucked from her chest; 1 brood per year

Eggs: 8–11; white without markings

Incubation: 24–27 days; female incubates

Fledging: 48–56 days; young feed themselves

Migration: complete to non-migrator in California

Food: aquatic insects

Compare: Male Gadwall is one of the few gray ducks. Look for its distinctive black rump.

Stan's Notes: A duck of shallow marshes. Consumes mostly plant material, dunking its head in water to feed rather than tipping forward, like other dabbling ducks. Frequently in pairs with other duck species. Nests within 300 feet (90 m) of water. Establishes pair bond in winter.

in flight

YEAR-ROUND

Great Blue Heron
Ardea herodias

Size: 42–48" (107–122 cm); up to 6' wingspan

Male: Tall and gray. Black eyebrows end in long plumes at the back of the head. Long yellow bill. Long feathers at the base of the neck drop down in a kind of necklace. Long legs.

Female: same as male

Juvenile: same as adults, but more brown than gray, with a black crown; lacks plumes

Nest: platform in a colony; male and female build; 1 brood per year

Eggs: 3–5; blue-green without markings

Incubation: 27–28 days; female and male incubate

Fledging: 56–60 days; male and female feed the young

Migration: non-migrator in California

Food: small fish, frogs, insects, snakes, baby birds

Compare: The Sandhill Crane (p. 355) has a red cap. Look for the long, yellow bill to help identify the Great Blue Heron.

Stan's Notes: One of the most common herons. Found in open water, from small ponds to large lakes. Stalks small fish in shallow water. Will strike at mice, squirrels and nearly anything it comes across. Red-winged Blackbirds will attack it to stop it from taking their babies out of the nest. In flight, it holds its neck in an S shape and slightly cups its wings, while the legs trail straight out behind. Nests in a colony of up to 100 birds. Nests in trees near or hanging over water. Barks like a dog when startled. Populations increase when birds north of California migrate to spend the winter.

in flight

rusty stain

in-flight
rusty stain

SUMMER
MIGRATION
WINTER

Sandhill Crane
Grus canadensis

Size: 42–48" (107–122 cm); up to 7' wingspan

Male: Elegant gray crane with long legs and neck. Wings and body often rust brown from mud staining. Scarlet-red cap. Yellow to red eyes.

Female: same as male

Juvenile: dull brown with yellow eyes; lacks a red cap

Nest: ground; female and male construct; 1 brood per year

Eggs: 2; olive with brown markings

Incubation: 28–32 days; female and male incubate

Fledging: 65 days; female and male feed the young

Migration: complete, to California, Mexico

Food: insects, fruit, worms, plants, amphibians

Compare: Great Blue Heron (p. 353) has a longer bill and holds its neck in an S shape during flight. Look for the scarlet-red cap to help identify the Sandhill Crane.

Stan's Notes: Preens mud into its feathers, staining its plumage rust brown (see insets). Gives a very loud and distinctive rattling call, often heard before the bird is seen. Flight is characteristic, with a faster upstroke, making the wings look like they're flicking in flight. Can fly at heights of over 10,000 feet (3,050 m). Nests on the ground in a large mound of aquatic vegetation. Performs a spectacular mating dance: The birds will face each other, then bow and jump into the air while making loud cackling sounds and flapping their wings. They will also flip sticks and grass into the air during their dance. Summers in northeastern California, spending winter in other parts of the state.

male

female

Calliope Hummingbird
Selasphorus calliope

SUMMER MIGRATION

Size: 3¼" (8 cm)

Male: Iridescent green head, back and tail. Breast and belly white to tan. V-shaped iridescent rosy red throat patch (gorget). A very short, thin bill and short tail compared with other hummingbirds. Wing tips reach to tip of tail.

Female: same as male, but thin, spotty throat patch

Juvenile: similar to female

Nest: cup; female builds; 1 brood per year

Eggs: 1–2; white without markings

Incubation: 15–17 days; female incubates

Fledging: 18–22 days; female feeds the young

Migration: complete, to Central and South America

Food: nectar, insects; will come to nectar feeders

Compare: Smaller than other hummingbirds. Look for a short thin bill, short tail and wing tips extending past the tail when perched. Female is similar to female Anna's Hummingbird (p. 363) and Rufous Hummingbird (p. 381), but it has a shorter, thinner bill and short tail.

Stan's Notes: The smallest bird in North America. Common in open forest and brushy areas in lower elevations of the state. A relatively quiet bird that will come to nectar feeders. During the breeding season, males can be heard zinging around while displaying for females. Females are hard to distinguish from other female hummingbirds. Often builds nest on branches of pine trees. Juvenile males obtain a partial throat patch by fall of their first year.

male

female

Costa's Hummingbird

Calypte costae

Size: 3½" (9 cm)

Male: Green back and nape. White belly. Light-green flanks. Dark crown, chin, throat and down the neck, like a handlebar mustache. White eyebrows. In direct sunlight, dark area around head reflects iridescent purple.

Female: same as male, without dark marks on head, has white marks around eyes, gray cheeks

Juvenile: similar to female

Nest: cup; female builds; 1 brood per year

Eggs: 2; white without markings

Incubation: 15–18 days; female incubates

Fledging: 20–23 days; female feeds young

Migration: partial migrator to non-migrator, to Mexico

Food: small insects, flower nectar; visits feeders

Compare: Smaller than the other hummers in California and has a shorter tail than most. Look for male's purple cap and mustache marks on throat. Identify the female by its gray cheeks and white markings around each eye. Wings extend just beyond tip of tail when perched.

Stan's Notes: Good lighting is needed to see the green iridescence. Some stay the winter if a consistent food source is available, such as a hummingbird feeder. Actively defends itself and is very territorial. Often perches, guarding territory and food supply. Gives a limited song, "tink-tink-tink," as it chases other hummers. Male performs an elaborate diving flight display to attract a mate. After mating, the female moves to her own territory to build nest and raise young.

male

female

Anna's Hummingbird

Calypte anna

YEAR-ROUND
SUMMER

Size: 4" (10 cm)

Male: Iridescent green body with dark head, chin and neck. In direct sunlight, the dark head shines a deep rose-red. Breast and belly are dull gray. White eye-ring.

Female: similar to male, but head reflects only a few red flecks instead of a complete rose-red

Juvenile: similar to female

Nest: cup; female builds; 2–3 broods per year

Eggs: 1–3; white without markings

Incubation: 14–19 days; female incubates

Fledging: 18–23 days; female feeds the young

Migration: partial migrator to non-migrator

Food: nectar, insects; will come to nectar feeders

Compare: Anna's is similar to other hummingbirds, but male has a completely dark head and a white eye-ring. Female has a few red flecks on the throat. Tail extends well beyond the wing tips when perched.

Stan's Notes: Common western hummingbird found from Baja, California to British Columbia. Males often seen on top of prominent perches looking around and calling. Quickly flies out to snap up insects or defend the territory from other hummers. An early nester. Female builds a tiny nest on chaparral-covered hillsides and in canyons. Feathers on head are black until seen in direct sun. Reflected sunlight turns the male's head bright rosy red. Apparently consumes more insects than other species of hummingbirds. Generally non-migratory; some may migrate.

Green-tailed Towhee

Pipilo chlorurus

Size: 7¼" (18.5 cm)

Male: A unique yellowish-green back, wings and tail. Dark-gray chest and face. Bright-white throat with black stripes. Rusty-red crown.

Female: same as male

Juvenile: olive-green with heavy streaking on breast and belly, lacks crown and throat markings of adult

Nest: cup; female and male construct; 1–2 broods per year

Eggs: 3–5; white with brown markings

Incubation: 12–14 days; female and male incubate

Fledging: 10–14 days; female and male feed young

Migration: complete, to Mexico and Central America

Food: insects, seeds, fruit

Compare: California Towhee (p. 187) is larger and lacks the rusty-red crown and bright white chin and throat. The Green-tailed's unusual color, short wings, long tail and large bill make it easy to identify.

Stan's Notes: A common bird of shrubby hillsides and sagebrush mountain slopes as high as 7,000 feet (2,150 m). Like other towhees, searches for insects and seeds, taking a little jump forward while kicking backward with both feet. Known to scurry away from trouble, jumping to ground without opening its wings and running across the ground.

Lewis's Woodpecker

Melanerpes lewis

YEAR-ROUND
MIGRATION
WINTER

Size: 10¾" (27.5 cm)

Male: Dull-green head and back. Distinctive gray collar and breast. Deep-red face and a light-red belly.

Female: same as male

Juvenile: similar to adult, with a brown head, lacking the red face

Nest: cavity; male and female excavate; 1 brood per year

Eggs: 4–8; white without markings

Incubation: 13–14 days; female and male incubate

Fledging: 28–34 days; female and male feed young

Migration: partial migrator to non-migrator; will move around to find food in winter

Food: insects, nuts, seeds, berries

Compare: Acorn Woodpecker (p. 67) has white on head and a red cap. Male Williamson's Sapsucker (p. 69) has a black back and large white wing patches.

Stan's Notes: Large and handsome woodpecker of western states. First scientifically collected in 1805 by Lewis and Clark in Montana. During breeding season, it feeds exclusively on adult insects rather than grubs, like other woodpeckers. Prefers open pine forests and areas with recent forest fires. Excavates in dead or soft wood. Uses same cavity year after year. Tends to mate for a long term. Doesn't migrate, but moves around in winter to search for food, such as pine nuts (seeds).

in flight

Green Heron
Butorides virescens

YEAR-ROUND
SUMMER
MIGRATION

Size: 16–22" (41–56 cm)

Male: Short and stocky. Blue-green back and rust-red neck and breast. Dark-green crest. Short legs are normally yellow but turn bright orange during the breeding season.

Female: same as male

Juvenile: similar to adults, with a bluish-gray back and white-streaked breast and neck

Nest: platform; female and male build; 2 broods per year

Eggs: 2–4; light green without markings

Incubation: 21–25 days; female and male incubate

Fledging: 35–36 days; female and male feed the young

Migration: complete to non-migrator in California

Food: small fish, aquatic insects, small amphibians

Compare: Great Blue Heron (p. 353) is larger. Green Heron lacks the long neck of other herons. Look for a small heron with a dark-green back and crest to identify the Green.

Stan's Notes: Often gives an explosive, rasping "skyew" call when startled. Holds its head close to its body, which sometimes makes it look like it doesn't have a neck. Waits on the shore or wades stealthily, hunting for small fish, aquatic insects and small amphibians. Places an object, such as an insect, on the water's surface to attract fish to catch. Nests in a tall tree, often a short distance from the water. The nest can be very high up in the tree. Babies give a loud ticking sound, like the ticktock of a clock.

female
p. 233

male

Wood Duck
Aix sponsa

YEAR-ROUND
SUMMER
WINTER

Size: 17–20" (43–51 cm)

Male: Small, highly ornamented dabbling duck. Mostly green head and crest patterned with black and white. Rusty chest and a white belly. Red eyes.

Female: brown duck with a bright-white eye-ring, not-so-obvious crest and blue patch on wings (speculum), often hidden

Juvenile: similar to female

Nest: cavity; female lines an old woodpecker cavity or a nest box in a tree; 1 brood per year

Eggs: 10–15; creamy white without markings

Incubation: 28–36 days; female incubates

Fledging: 56–68 days; female teaches the young to feed

Migration: non-migrator to partial in California

Food: aquatic insects, plants, seeds

Compare: Male Northern Shoveler (p. 375) is larger with a long wide bill. Male Green-winged Teal (p. 219) lacks Wood Duck's showy colors.

Stan's Notes: A duck of quiet, shallow backwater ponds. Nearly extinct around 1900 due to overhunting, but doing well now. Nests in tree cavity or nest box. Seen flying in forests or perching on high branches. Female takes off with a loud squealing call and enters the nest cavity from full flight. Lays some eggs in a neighboring nest (egg dumping), resulting in more than 20 eggs in some clutches. Hatchlings stay in nest for 24 hours, then jump from as high as 60 feet (18 m) to the ground or water to follow their mother. They never return to the nest.

female
p. 247

male

YEAR-ROUND

Mallard
Anas platyrhynchos

Size: 19–21" (48–53 cm)

Male: Large, bulbous green head, white necklace and rust-brown or chestnut chest. Gray-and-white sides. Yellow bill. Orange legs and feet.

Female: brown with an orange-and-black bill and blue-and-white wing mark (speculum)

Juvenile: same as female but with a yellow bill

Nest: ground; female builds; 1 brood per year

Eggs: 7–10; greenish to whitish, unmarked

Incubation: 26–30 days; female incubates

Fledging: 42–52 days; female leads the young to food

Migration: non-migrator to partial migrator in California

Food: seeds, plants, aquatic insects; will come to ground feeders offering corn

Compare: Male Northern Shoveler (p. 375) has a white chest with rusty sides and a very large, spoon-shaped bill. Breeding male Northern Pintail (p. 249) has long tail feathers and a brown head. Male Red-breasted Merganser (p. 377) has a shaggy crest and orange bill.

Stan's Notes: A familiar dabbling duck of lakes and ponds. Also found in rivers, streams and some backyards. Tips forward to feed on vegetation on the bottom of shallow water. The name "Mallard" comes from the Latin word *masculus,* meaning "male," referring to the male's habit of taking no part in raising the young. Male and female have white underwings and white tails, but only the male has black central tail feathers that curl upward. Unlike the female, the male doesn't quack.

female
p. 245

male

Northern Shoveler
Anas clypeata

Size: 19–21" (48–53 cm)

Male: Medium-size duck with an iridescent green head, rust sides, white chest. Extraordinarily large, spoon-shaped bill, almost always held pointed toward the water.

Female: brown and black all over, green wing patch (speculum) and a large spoon-shaped bill

Juvenile: same as female

Nest: ground; female builds; 1 brood per year

Eggs: 9–12; olive without markings

Incubation: 22–25 days; female incubates

Fledging: 30–60 days; female leads the young to food

Migration: complete to non-migrator, to California, Mexico, and Central America

Food: aquatic insects, plants

Compare: Male Mallard (p. 373) is similar, but it lacks the large spoon-shaped bill. Larger than male Wood Duck (p. 371) and lacks the Wood Duck's Crest.

Stan's Notes: One of several species of shovelers. Called "Shoveler" due to the peculiar, shovel-like shape of its bill. Given the common name "Northern" because it is the only species of these ducks in North America. Seen in shallow wetlands, ponds and small lakes in flocks of 5–10 birds. Flocks fly in tight formation. Swims low in water, pointing its large bill toward the water as if it's too heavy to lift. Usually swims in tight circles while feeding. Feeds mainly by filtering tiny aquatic insects and plants from the surface of the water with its bill. Female gathers plant material and forms it into a nest a short distance from the water. Winters in California where it can find water.

female
p. 263

male

Red-breasted Merganser

Mergus serrator

MIGRATION
WINTER

Size: 23" (58 cm)

Male: A shaggy green head and crest. Prominent white collar. Rusty breast. Black-and-white body. Long orange bill.

Female: overall brown to gray with a shaggy reddish head and crest, long orange bill

Juvenile: similar to female

Nest: ground; female builds; 1 brood per year

Eggs: 5–10; olive-green without markings

Incubation: 29–30 days; female incubates

Fledging: 55–65 days; female feeds young

Migration: complete, to coastal California, Mexico and Central America

Food: fish, aquatic insects

Compare: The male Hooded Merganser (p. 85) has a large white patch on the head, unlike the green head of male Red-breasted Merganser.

Stan's Notes: This duck is a very fast flier, clocked at up to 100 miles (161 km) per hour. Frequently seen flying low across the water. Needs a long run for takeoff with wings flapping to get airborne. Serrated bill helps it catch slippery fish. Usually is a silent duck. Male sometimes gives a soft, catlike meow. Female gives a harsh "krrr-croak." Doesn't breed before 2 years of age. The male abandons the female just after eggs are laid. Females often share nests. Breeds across Alaska and northern Canada. The young leave the nest within 24 hours of hatching, never to return.

male

female

Allen's Hummingbird

Selasphorus sasin

YEAR-ROUND
SUMMER
MIGRATION

Size: 3¾" (9.5 cm)

Male: Rusty-orange cheeks, chest, belly, rump and tail. Iridescent green cap, back and upper surface of wings. Long, thin dark bill. Small white patch in center of breast, just under throat patch (gorget). A nearly black gorget, turning reddish-orange in direct sunlight.

Female: similar to male, but much less orange, solid green back and tail, small reddish-orange flecks on throat, lacks the large throat patch

Juvenile: similar to female, with a white chin

Nest: cup; female builds; 1–2 broods per year

Eggs: 2; white without markings

Incubation: 17–22 days; female incubates

Fledging: 22–25 days; female feeds young

Migration: complete, to Mexico and Central America

Food: nectar, insects; will come to nectar feeders

Compare: Male Rufous (p. 381) has an orange back and crown. Rufous and Allen's females are nearly identical, but Rufous is usually seen during migration and winter.

Stan's Notes: Male performs for perching female, swooping up to 75 feet (23 m) in a J shape, giving a buzzing call at the bottom. After mating, female builds a small nest of plant fibers on the top of a tree limb. She camouflages the outside with lichen bits and binds it with spider silk, often completing it in 10–12 days. Hummingbirds often lay only two eggs. Female defends nest area from most birds. Adult males migrate first in fall. Females and young follow a month later.

male

female

Rufous Hummingbird
Selasphorus rufus

MIGRATION
WINTER

Size: 3¾" (9.5 cm)

Male: Tiny burnt-orange bird with a black throat patch (gorget) that reflects orange-red in sunlight. White chest. Green-to-tan flanks.

Female: same as male, but lacking the throat patch

Juvenile: similar to female

Nest: cup; female builds; 1–2 broods per year

Eggs: 1–3; white without markings

Incubation: 14–17 days; female incubates

Fledging: 21–26 days; female feeds young

Migration: complete, to California, Central America and South America

Food: nectar, insects; will come to nectar feeders

Compare: Identify it by the unique orange-red (rufous) color. Very similar to Allen's Hummingbird (p. 379), but male Allen's has a green back and cap. Females are nearly identical, but the Allen's is seen in summer.

Stan's Notes: This is a bold, hardy hummer. Frequently seen well out of its normal range in the western U.S., showing up along the East Coast. Visits hummingbird feeders in your yard during migration. Does not sing, but it will chatter or buzz to communicate. Weighing just 2–3 grams, it takes about five average-size hummingbirds to equal the weight of one chickadee. The heart beats up to an incredible 1,260 times per minute. Male performs a spectacular pendulum-like flight over the perched female. After mating, the female will fly off to build a nest and raise young, without any help from her mate. Constructs a soft, flexible nest that expands to accommodate the growing young. Doesn't nest in California.

female
p. 433

male

Bullock's Oriole

Icterus bullockii

SUMMER

Size: 8" (20 cm)

Male: Bright-orange-and-black bird. Black crown, eye line, nape, chin, back and wings with a bold white patch on wings.

Female: dull-yellow overall, pale-white belly, white wing bars on gray-to-black wings

Juvenile: similar to female

Nest: pendulous; female and male build; 1 brood per year

Eggs: 4–6; pale white to gray, brown markings

Incubation: 12–14 days; female incubates

Fledging: 12–14 days; female and male feed young

Migration: complete, to Central and South America

Food: insects, berries, nectar; visits nectar feeders

Compare: A handsome bird. Look for male Bullock's bright orange and black markings, and the thin black line running through the eyes.

Stan's Notes: So closely related to Baltimore Orioles of the eastern U.S., at one time both were considered a single species. Interbreeds with Baltimores where their ranges overlap. Most common in the state where cottonwood trees grow along rivers and other wetlands. Also found at edges of clearings, in city parks, on farms and along irrigation ditches. Hanging, sock-like nest is constructed of plant fibers such as inner bark of junipers and willows.

female
p. 435

male

Hooded Oriole
Icterus cucullatus

SUMMER

Size: 8" (20 cm)

Male: Orange-yellow head, nape, chest, rump and belly. Black face, chin, throat, bill and eyes. Large white wing bar. Dark wings and tail.

Female: dull yellow with gray wings and back

Juvenile: similar to adult of the same sex

Nest: pendulous; female and male construct; 1–2 broods per year

Eggs: 3–5; dull white with brown markings

Incubation: 12–14 days; female incubates

Fledging: 12–14 days; female and male feed young

Migration: complete, to Central and South America

Food: insects, fruit, nectar

Compare: Male Bullock's Oriole (p. 383) is the same size but has a black crown and nape. Male Scott's Oriole (p. 437) is larger and has a black head and chest.

Stan's Notes: A bird of tree-lined creeks and streams, palm groves, mesquite and arid scrub, often near suburbs. Male courts female with bows while hopping around her, singing a soft song. Points his bill skyward (like many birds in the blackbird family). Female will respond with a similar dance. Constructs an unusual sock-like nest, hung from a twig or woven through a palm leaf. Entrance often near the top, but can be on the side. Takes 3–7 days to build nest of wiry green grass, shredded palm leaves or yucca fibers. Some repair and reuse nests. Sips flower nectar, but not like hummingbirds. Often slices into the base of a flower, bypassing its natural entrance. Young are fed a regurgitate of insects and nectar the first 5–7 days of life.

female
p. 177

male

Black-headed Grosbeak
Pheucticus melanocephalus

SUMMER
MIGRATION

Size: 8" (20 cm)

Male: Stocky bird with burnt-orange chest, neck and rump. Black head, tail and wings. Irregularly shaped white wing patches. Large bill, with upper bill darker than lower.

Female: appears like an overgrown sparrow, overall brown with a lighter breast and belly, large two-toned bill, prominent white eyebrows, yellow wing linings, as seen in flight

Juvenile: similar to adult of the same sex

Nest: cup; female builds; 1 brood per year

Eggs: 3–4; pale green or bluish, brown markings

Incubation: 11–13 days; female and male incubate

Fledging: 11–13 days; female and male feed young

Migration: complete, to Mexico, Central America and South America

Food: seeds, insects, fruit; comes to seed feeders

Compare: Male Bullock's Oriole (p. 383) has more white on the wings than the male Black-headed Grosbeak. Look for Black-headed's large bicolored bill.

Stan's Notes: A cosmopolitan bird that nests in a wide variety of habitats. Both the male and female sing and will aggressively defend the nest against intruders. Song is very similar to American Robin's (p. 319) and Western Tanager's (p. 431), making it hard to tell them apart by song. Populations increasing in California and across the U.S.

male

female

Varied Thrush

Ixoreus naevius

YEAR-ROUND
MIGRATION
WINTER

Size: 9½" (24 cm)

Male: Potbellied robin-like bird with orange eyebrows, chin, breast and wing bars. Head, neck and back are gray to blue. Black breast band and eye mark.

Female: browner version of male, lacking the black breast band

Juvenile: similar to female

Nest: cup; female builds; 1–2 broods per year

Eggs: 3–5; pale blue with brown markings

Incubation: 12–14 days; female and male incubate

Fledging: 10–15 days; female and male feed young

Migration: complete, to California; non-migrator in parts of California

Food: insects, fruit

Compare: Similar size and shape as American Robin (p. 319), but the Varied Thrush has a warm-orange breast unlike the red breast of Robin. Male Thrush has a distinctive black breast band.

Stan's Notes: An intriguing-looking bird. Nests in Alaska, Canada and the mountains of the U.S. Northwest. Prefers moist coniferous forests. It is most common in dense, older coniferous forests in high elevations. Moves to lower elevations in the winter, where it is often seen in towns, orchards or thickets. Seen during winter in flocks of up to 20 birds. Individual Varied Thrush birds sometimes fly eastward in winter, and they can show up in nearly any state before returning to the West Coast for breeding.

male

female
p. 131

yellow
male

YEAR-ROUND

House Finch
Haemorhous mexicanus

Size: 5" (13 cm)

Male: Small finch with a red-to-orange face, throat, chest and rump. Brown cap. Brown marking behind eyes. White belly with brown streaks. Brown wings with white streaks.

Female: brown with a heavily streaked white chest

Juvenile: similar to female

Nest: cup, sometimes in cavities; female builds; 2 broods per year

Eggs: 4–5; pale blue, lightly marked

Incubation: 12–14 days; female incubates

Fledging: 15–19 days; female and male feed the young

Migration: non-migrator; moves around to find food

Food: seeds, fruit, leaf buds; visits seed feeders and feeders that offer grape jelly

Compare: The male Vermilion Flycatcher (p. 393) has a black nape, back and wings.

Stan's Notes: Very social bird, visits feeders in small flocks. Likes to nest in hanging flower baskets. Male sings a loud, cheerful warbling song. Historically it occurred from the Pacific to the Rockies, with only a few reaching the eastern side. Birds introduced to Long Island, New York, in the 1940s have populated the entire eastern U.S. Now found across the U.S. Suffers from a disease that causes the eyes to crust, resulting in blindness and death. Rarely, some males are yellow (see inset) instead of red, probably due to poor diet.

female
p. 297

male

Vermilion Flycatcher

Pyrocephalus rubinus

YEAR-ROUND
SUMMER
WINTER

Size: 6" (15 cm)

Male: A stunningly beautiful bird with a crimson-red head, crest, chin, breast and belly. Black nape, back, wings and tail. Thick black line running through eyes. Thin black bill.

Female: gray head, neck and back, nearly white chin and breast, pink belly to undertail, black tail, thin black bill

Juvenile: similar to female, lacks a pink undertail

Nest: cup; female builds; 1–2 broods per year

Eggs: 2–4; white with brown markings

Incubation: 14–16 days; female and male incubate

Fledging: 14–16 days; female and male feed young

Migration: complete migrator to non-migrator in parts of southern California

Food: insects (mainly bees)

Compare: The unique bright crimson plumage with black wings make this bird easy to identify.

Stan's Notes: A uniquely colored flycatcher that is often found in open areas with shrubs and small trees close to water. Feeds mainly on insects, with bees making up a large part of its diet. Will perch on a thin branch, pumping tail up and down while waiting for an aerial insect. Flies out to snatch it, then returns to the perch. Drops to the ground for terrestrial insects. Male raises its crest, fluffs chest feathers, fans tail and sings a song during a fluttery flight to court females. Female builds a shallow nest of twigs and grasses and lines it with downy plant material. Male feeds female during incubation and brooding.

breeding

winter

YEAR-ROUND
SUMMER

Snowy Plover
Charadrius nivosus

Size: 6¼" (15.5 cm)

Male: Small shorebird with pale white face, nape, chin, chest, belly and undertail. Black patch on forehead, each side of neck and behind each eye. Small dark bill. Gray legs and feet. Winter plumage lacks black markings.

Female: same as male

Juvenile: similar to winter adult

Nest: ground; male builds; 1–2 broods per year

Eggs: 2–3; buff white with brown markings

Incubation: 25–32 days; male and female incubate

Fledging: 30–32 days; male and female teach young what to eat

Migration: partial to non-migrator, from inland to the California coast and Mexico

Food: insects, worms, tiny fish

Compare: Killdeer (p. 197) is larger with 2 distinct black bands around neck and upper chest. The breeding Black-bellied Plover (p. 73) is larger with a black belly, chest and face.

Stan's Notes: The smallest, whitest North American plover. Often on beaches, mud and salt flats, fields and farms. In pairs during breeding season, groups at other times. Unique feeding behavior. Runs a few quick steps, then stops to look for moving prey. Vibrates legs and feet to scare up prey. Male displays to female at nest. Bows forward, points bill at nest, raises wings and ruffles feathers. Builds several nests, but uses one. Female leaves six days after eggs hatch. Male cares for young for a month. One in three females mates again.

in flight

breeding

winter

Bonaparte's Gull
Chroicocephalus philadelphia

MIGRATION
WINTER

Size: 13½" (34.5 cm); up to 3' wingspan

Male: Mostly white during breeding season (April to August) with gray upper surface of wings and back. Black head, small black bill and white crescent marks around eyes. Black tips of wings and tail, seen in flight. Winter lacks a black head and has a dark ear spot.

Female: same as male

Juvenile: similar to winter male

Nest: platform; female and male construct; 1–2 broods per year

Eggs: 2–4; light brown with brown markings

Incubation: 20–24 days; female and male incubate

Fledging: 21–25 days; female and male feed young

Migration: complete, to coastal California and Mexico

Food: aquatic and terrestrial insects, fish

Compare: California Gull (p. 403) and Western Gull (p. 405) are larger and lack the breeding Bonaparte's black head. Look for the small black bill to help identify Bonaparte's Gull.

Stan's Notes: Rarely with other gull species, presumably due to its small size. California is home to some of the highest concentrations of this species in the U.S. Rarely found away from the coast during winter, but on lakes and rivers during migration. Said to resemble a tern species due to its small size, short thin bill and swift flight. It nests across Canada and southern Alaska where there is water. Builds its own nest or takes an abandoned nest in a tree, mainly conifers. Takes two years for young to obtain adult plumage.

in flight

breeding

juvenile

winter

Ring-billed Gull
Larus delawarensis

MIGRATION
WINTER

Size: 18–20" (45–51 cm); up to 4' wingspan

Male: White with gray wings, black wing tips spotted with white, and a white tail, seen in flight (inset). Yellow bill with a black ring near the tip. Yellowish legs and feet. In winter, the back of the head and the nape of the neck are speckled brown.

Female: same as male

Juvenile: white with brown speckles and a brown tip of tail; mostly dark bill

Nest: ground; female and male construct; 1 brood per year

Eggs: 2–4; off-white with brown markings

Incubation: 20–21 days; female and male incubate

Fledging: 20–40 days; female and male feed the young

Migration: complete, to California and Mexico

Food: insects, fish; scavenges for food

Compare: California Gull (p. 403) is larger and has a larger bill with a red-and-black mark near the tip; it also has dark eyes, compared with Ring-billed's light-colored eyes. Smaller than Western Gull (p. 405)

Stan's Notes: A common gull of garbage dumps and parking lots. It's expanding its range and remaining farther north longer during winter due to successful scavenging in cities. Hundreds of these birds often flock together. A three-year gull with different plumages in each of its first three years. Attains the ring on its bill after the first winter and adult plumage in the third year. Defends a small area around the nest, usually only a few feet.

winter

in flight

breeding

in flight
juvenile

Western Gull
Larus occidentalis

YEAR-ROUND

Size: 24" (60 cm); up to 5' wingspan

Male: Mostly white with a gray back. Gray upper surface of wings with white edges and black wing tips. Large yellow bill with an orange dot near end of lower mandible. Winter has some fine brown streaking on cap and nape.

Female: same as male

Juvenile: light brown overall with a dark band on the end of tail, dark bill

Nest: ground; female and male construct; 1 brood per year

Eggs: 1–4; light brown without markings

Incubation: 24–29 days; female and male incubate

Fledging: 42–48 days; female and male feed young

Migration: non-migrator; will move up and down the coast to find food during winter

Food: fish, aquatic insects, shellfish

Compare: California Gull (p. 403) is smaller and has a red-and-black mark near the tip of lower mandible. The Bonaparte's Gull (p. 399) is much smaller and has a small black bill.

Stan's Notes: A large gull of rocky shores and coastal cliffs. It has learned to drop shellfish from the air onto rocks to break them open. Nests in large colonies with other shorebirds, building a grass nest near water or in a man-made structure. One parent incubates and one stands guard. Performs distraction display to draw danger away from nest. In hot weather, soaks its belly feathers to transport water to cool eggs. A four-year gull, attaining breeding plumage at four years.

in flight

Snowy Egret
Egretta thula

YEAR-ROUND
SUMMER
MIGRATION

Size: 22–26" (56–66 cm); up to 3½' wingspan

Male: All-white bird with black bill. Black legs. Bright-yellow feet. Long feather plumes on head, neck and back during breeding season.

Female: same as male

Juvenile: similar to adult, but backs of legs are yellow

Nest: platform; female and male build; 1 brood per year

Eggs: 3–5; light blue-green without markings

Incubation: 20–24 days; female and male incubate

Fledging: 28–30 days; female and male feed the young

Migration: non-migrator to partial in California

Food: aquatic insects, small fish

Compare: Much smaller than the Great Egret (p. 411), which has a yellow bill and black feet. Look for the black bill and yellow feet of Snowy Egret to help identify.

Stan's Notes: Common in wetlands and often seen with other egrets. Colonies may include up to several hundred nests. Nests are low in shrubs 5–10-feet (1.5–3 m) tall or constructs a nest on the ground, usually mixed among other egret and heron nests. Chicks hatch days apart (asynchronous), leading to starvation of last to hatch. Will actively "hunt" prey by moving around quickly, stirring up small fish and aquatic insects with its feet. In the breeding state, a yellow patch at the base of the bill and the yellow feet turn orange-red. Was hunted to near extinction in the late 1800s for its feathers.

white
morph

blue morph

juvenile

Ross's Goose

in flight

Snow Goose
Chen caerulescens

MIGRATION
WINTER

Size: 25–38" (64–97 cm); up to 4½' wingspan

Male: White morph has black wing tips and varying patches of black and brown. Blue morph has a white head and a gray breast and back. Both morphs have a pink bill and legs.

Female: same as male

Juvenile: overall dull gray with a dark bill

Nest: ground; female builds; 1 brood per year

Eggs: 3–5; white without markings

Incubation: 23–25 days; female incubates

Fledging: 45–49 days; female and male teach the young to feed

Migration: complete migrator, to California and Mexico

Food: aquatic insects and plants

Compare: Tundra Swan (p. 413) is much larger and lacks the black wing tips. White Pelican (p. 415) shares the black wing tips, but has an enormous bill.

Stan's Notes: This bird occurs in light (white) and dark (blue) color morphs. The white morph is more common than the blue. A bird of wide-open fields, wetlands and lakes of any size. It has a thick, serrated bill, which helps it to grab and pull up plants. Breeds in large colonies on the northern tundra in Canada. Female starts to breed at 2–3 years. Older females produce more eggs and are more successful at reproduction than younger females. Seen by the thousands during migration and in winter. Has a classic goose-like call. The Ross's Goose (see inset) is slightly smaller with a much smaller pink bill. Often see with Ross's Geese and Sandhill Cranes.

in flight

Great Egret
Ardea alba

YEAR-ROUND
SUMMER
MIGRATION

Size: 36–40" (91–102 cm); up to 4½' wingspan

Male: Tall, thin, all-white bird with a long neck and a long, pointed yellow bill. Black, stilt-like legs and black feet.

Female: same as male

Juvenile: same as adults

Nest: platform; male and female construct; 1 brood per year

Eggs: 2–3; light blue without markings

Incubation: 23–26 days; female and male incubate

Fledging: 43–49 days; female and male feed the young

Migration: non-migrator to partial in California

Food: small fish, aquatic insects, frogs, crayfish

Compare: The Snowy Egret (p. 407) is much smaller, with yellow feet and a black bill. Great Blue Heron (p. 353) has a similar shape, but is larger in size and is not white.

Stan's Notes: Slowly stalks shallow ponds, lakes and wetlands in search of small fish to spear with its long, sharp bill. Gives a loud, dry croak if disturbed or when squabbling for a nest site at the colony. The name "Egret" comes from the French word *aigrette,* meaning "ornamental tufts of plumes." The plumes grow near the tail during the breeding season. Hunted to near extinction in the 1800s and early 1900s for its long plumes, which were used to decorate women's hats. Today, the egret is a protected species.

juvenile

in flight

Tundra Swan
Cygnus columbianus

MIGRATION
WINTER

Size:	50–54" (127–137 cm); up to 5½' wingspan
Male:	Large all-white swan. Black bill, legs and feet. Small yellow mark in front of each eye.
Female:	same as male
Juvenile:	same size as adult with gray plumage, pinkish-gray bill
Nest:	ground; female and male construct; 1 brood per year
Eggs:	4–5; creamy white without markings
Incubation:	35–40 days; female and male incubate
Fledging:	60–70 days; female and male feed the young
Migration:	complete, to parts of California
Food:	plants, aquatic insects
Compare:	The Snow Goose (p. 409) is much smaller and has black wing tips. Look for the black bill and legs of Tundra Swan.

Stan's Notes: Nests on the tundra of northern Canada and Alaska, hence its common name. Migrates diagonally across North America to reach wintering grounds on the East Coast. Flies in large V-shaped wedges. Gathers in large numbers of several thousand during the winter. Often seen in large family groups of 20 or more individuals. Gives a high-pitched, whistle-like call. Young are easy to distinguish by their gray plumage and pinkish bills.

breeding

in flight

chick-feeding
adult

American White Pelican
Pelecanus erythrorhynchos

SUMMER
MIGRATION
WINTER

Size: 60–64" (152–163 cm); up to 9' wingspan

Male: Large white pelican with an enormous bright-yellow-to-orange bill. Yellow legs and feet. Black wing tips and trailing edge of wings. Breeding plumage has a bright-orange bill, legs and feet. Chick-feeding adult (an adult that is feeding young) has a gray-black crown.

Female: same as male

Juvenile: duller white than adult, with a brownish head and neck

Nest: ground, scraped-out depression rimmed with dirt; female and male build; 1 brood per year

Eggs: 1–3; white without markings

Incubation: 29–36 days; male and female incubate

Fledging: 60–70 days; female and male feed the young

Migration: complete to partial migrator

Food: fish

Compare: Very similar to the Brown Pelican (p. 271), only white with a yellow or orange bill.

Stan's Notes: Often seen in large groups on the larger lakes and reservoirs of California. Doesn't dive to catch fish, like coastal Brown Pelicans. Instead, groups swim and dip their bills simultaneously into water to scoop up fish. Groups fly in a large V, often gliding, followed by simultaneous flapping. Large flocks swirl on columns of rising warm air (thermals) on hot days. Breeding adults typically grow a flat, fibrous plate on the upper bill, which drops off after the eggs hatch. Usually silent; gives short grunts at the nesting colony.

male

female

Lesser Goldfinch
Spinus psaltria

YEAR-ROUND
SUMMER

Size: 4½" (11 cm)

Male: Striking bright yellow beneath from chin to base of tail. Black head, tail and wings. White patches on wings. Eastern variety has a black back. Western has a green back.

Female: dull yellow underneath, lacks a black head and back

Juvenile: same as female

Nest: cup; female builds; 1–2 broods per year

Eggs: 4–5; pale blue without markings

Incubation: 10–12 days; female incubates

Fledging: 12–14 days; female and male feed young

Migration: partial to non-migrator; will move around the state to find food

Food: seeds, insects; will come to seed feeders

Compare: The male American Goldfinch (p. 423) is slightly larger and has a yellow back, unlike the greenish back of male eastern Lesser Goldfinch or the black back of male western Lesser Goldfinch. The male Lawrence's Goldfinch (p. 421) is mostly gray with a black chin.

Stan's Notes: The western males have greenish backs, while males in the eastern range (Texas) have entirely black heads and backs. Some females are extremely pale. Prefers forest edges with a consistent water source. Unlike many other birds, its diet is about 96 percent seed, even during peak insect season. Will come to seed feeders. Late summer nesters. Male feeds the incubating female by regurgitating seeds. Pairs stay together all winter. Winter flocks can number in the hundreds.

Lawrence's Goldfinch
Spinus lawrencei

Size: 4¾" (12 cm)

Male: Pale gray bird with bright yellow highlights on breast, wing bars and rump. Black face and chin. Dark wings and tail.

Female: similar to male, not as bright yellow, lacks the black face and chin

Juvenile: similar to female

Nest: cup; female builds; 1–2 broods per year

Eggs: 3–6; pale blue without markings

Incubation: 12–14 days; female and male incubate

Fledging: 11–13 days; male and female feed young

Migration: partial to non-migrator, to southern California and northern Mexico

Food: seeds, insects

Compare: The Lesser Goldfinch (p. 417) has more yellow and lacks the gray back and black chin of male Lawrence's. The breeding male American Goldfinch (p. 423) has much more yellow and lacks the male Lawrence's black chin.

Stan's Notes: A finch of wetlands, chaparral and arid areas with water nearby. Strong association with water and plentiful seed crops from native plants. Clings to seed heads and plucks ripe seeds. Also feeds on the ground, taking insects with fallen seeds. Well known for its song, mainly imitations of other bird calls. Returns in April and May to breeding grounds. Usually nests near other Lawrence's. Male feeds nesting female and young. When not breeding, often in flocks with other finches. Frequently seen bathing in shallow water.

male

winter
male

female

American Goldfinch
Spinus tristis

YEAR-ROUND
WINTER

Size: 5" (13 cm)

Male: Canary-yellow finch with a black forehead and tail. Black wings with white wing bars. White rump. No markings on the chest. Winter male is similar to the female.

Female: dull olive-yellow plumage with brown wings; lacks a black forehead

Juvenile: same as female

Nest: cup; female builds; 1 brood per year

Eggs: 4–6; pale blue without markings

Incubation: 10–12 days; female incubates

Fledging: 11–17 days; female and male feed the young

Migration: non-migrator to partial; small flocks of up to 20 birds move around to find food

Food: seeds, insects; will come to seed feeders

Compare: Male western and eastern Lesser Goldfinch (p. 417) have a greenish or black back, respectively. Male Lawrence's Goldfinch (p. 421) has a black chin. The Pine Siskin (p. 129) and female House Finch (p. 131) have streaked breasts. Male Yellow Warbler (p. 429) is all yellow with orange streaks on breast. Male Wilson's Warbler (p. 419) lacks black wings.

Stan's Notes: Most often found in open fields, scrubby areas and woodlands. Enjoys Nyjer seed in feeders. Lines its nest with the silky down from wild thistle. Almost always in small flocks. Twitters while it flies. Flight is roller coaster-like. Often called Wild Canary due to the male's canary-colored plumage. Male sings a pleasant, high-pitched song.

Common Yellowthroat

Geothlypis trichas

YEAR-ROUND
SUMMER
MIGRATION

Size: 5" (13 cm)

Male: Olive-brown with a bright-yellow throat and chest, a white belly and a distinctive black mask outlined in white. Long, thin, pointed black bill.

Female: similar to male but lacks a black mask

Juvenile: same as female

Nest: cup; female builds; 2 broods per year

Eggs: 3–5; white with brown markings

Incubation: 11–12 days; female incubates

Fledging: 10–11 days; female and male feed the young

Migration: non-migrator to partial in California

Food: insects

Compare: The male American Goldfinch (p. 423) has a black forehead and wings. Male Yellow Warbler (p. 429) has fine orange streaks on chest and lacks the black mask. The Yellow-rumped Warbler (p. 287) only has patches of yellow and lacks the yellow chest of the Yellowthroat. Male Wilson's Warbler (p. 419) lacks the Yellowthroat's black mask.

Stan's Notes: A common warbler of open fields and marshes. Sings a cheerful, well-known "witchity-witchity-witchity-witchity" song from deep within tall grasses. Male sings from prominent perches and while he hunts. He performs a curious courtship display, bouncing in and out of tall grass while singing a mating song. Female builds a nest low to the ground. Young remain dependent on their parents longer than most other warblers. A frequent cowbird host.

Orange-crowned Warbler
Oreothlypis celata

YEAR-ROUND
SUMMER
MIGRATION
WINTER

Size: 5" (13 cm)

Male: An overall pale-yellow bird with a dark line through the eyes. Faint streaking on sides and chest. Tawny-orange crown, often invisible. Small thin bill.

Female: same as male, but very slightly duller, often indistinguishable in the field

Juvenile: same as adults

Nest: cup; female builds; 1–2 broods per year

Eggs: 3–6; white with brown markings

Incubation: 12–14 days; female incubates

Fledging: 8–10 days; female and male feed young

Migration: non-migrator to partial in California, to Mexico and Central America

Food: insects, fruit, nectar

Compare: Yellow Warbler (p. 429) is brighter yellow with orange streaking on the male's chest. Wilson's Warbler (p. 419) is also brighter yellow with a distinct black cap. Male Common Yellowthroat (p. 425) has a distinctive black mask.

Stan's Notes: This widespread warbler can be seen year-round in western California but is frequently seen more during migration when large groups move together. Builds a bulky, well-concealed nest on the ground with nest rim at ground level. Known to drink flower nectar. The orange crown tends to be hidden and is rarely seen in the field. A widespread breeder, from western Texas to Alaska and across Canada.

Yellow Warbler
Setophaga petechia

**SUMMER
WINTER**

Size: 5" (13 cm)

Male: Yellow with thin orange streaks on the chest and belly. Long, pointed dark bill.

Female: same as male but lacks orange streaks

Juvenile: similar to female but much duller

Nest: cup; female builds; 1 brood per year

Eggs: 4–5; white with brown markings

Incubation: 11–12 days; female incubates

Fledging: 10–12 days; female and male feed the young

Migration: complete, to southern California, Mexico, and Central and South America

Food: insects

Compare: Look for orange streaking on chest of male. Orange-crowned Warbler (p. 427) is paler yellow. Male American Goldfinch (p. 423) has black wings and forehead. The female Yellow Warbler is similar to the female American Goldfinch (p. 423), but it lacks white wing bars. Similar to male Wilson's Warbler (p. 419), which has a black cap, and lacks streaks on chest and belly.

Stan's Notes: A widespread and common warbler in the state, seen in gardens and shrubby areas near water. A prolific insect eater, gleaning caterpillars and other insects from tree leaves. Male sings a string of notes that sound like "sweet, sweet, sweet, I'm-so-sweet!" Begins to migrate in August. Returns in late April. Males arrive in spring before females to claim territories. Migrates at night in mixed flocks of warblers. Rests and feeds during the day.

male

non-breeding
male

female

SUMMER
MIGRATION

Western Tanager
Piranga ludoviciana

Size: 7¼" (18.5 cm)

Male: A canary-yellow bird with a red head. Black back, tail, wings. One white and one yellow wing bar. Non-breeding lacks the red head.

Female: duller than male, lacking the red head

Juvenile: similar to female

Nest: cup; female builds; 1 brood per year

Eggs: 3–5; light blue with brown markings

Incubation: 14–18 days; female incubates

Fledging: 16–20 days; female and male feed young

Migration: complete, to Mexico and Central America

Food: insects, fruit

Compare: Male American Goldfinch (p. 423) has a black forehead and lacks breeding Western male's red head. Female Bullock's and Scott's Orioles (pp. 383 and 437) lack female Western's single yellow wing bars.

Stan's Notes: The male is stunning in its breeding plumage. Feeds mainly on insects, such as bees, wasps, cicadas and grasshoppers, and to a lesser degree on fruit. The male feeds the female while she incubates. Female builds a cup nest in a horizontal fork of a coniferous tree, well away from the main trunk, 20–40 feet (6–12 m) aboveground. This is the farthest-nesting tanager species, reaching far up into the Northwest Territories of Canada. An early fall migrant, often seen migrating in late July (when non-breeding males lack red heads). Seen in many habitats during migration.

female

male
p. 383

Bullock's Oriole
Icterus bullockii

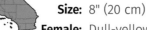

SUMMER

Size:	8" (20 cm)
Female:	Dull-yellow head and chest. Gray-to-black wings with white wing bars. A pale-white belly. Gray back, as seen in flight.
Male:	bright-orange-and-black bird with a bold white patch on wings
Juvenile:	similar to female
Nest:	pendulous; female and male build; 1 brood per year
Eggs:	4–6; pale white to gray, brown markings
Incubation:	12–14 days; female incubates
Fledging:	12–14 days; female and male feed young
Migration:	complete, to Central and South America
Food:	insects, berries, nectar; visits nectar feeders
Compare:	Female Scott's Oriole (p. 437) is larger and lacks the pale-white belly. Female Western Tanager (p. 431) has a black back unlike the female Oriole's gray back. Female Hooded Oriole (p. 435) is the same size, but lacks the pale white belly. Look for the overall dull-yellow and gray appearance of the female Bullock's Oriole.

Stan's Notes: So closely related to Baltimore Orioles of the eastern U.S., at one time both were considered a single species. Interbreeds with Baltimores where their ranges overlap. Most common in the state where cottonwood trees grow alongside rivers and other wetlands. Also found at edges of clearings, in city parks, on farms, and along irrigation ditches. Hanging sock-like nest is constructed of plant fibers such as inner bark of junipers and willows.

433

male
p. 385

female

Hooded Oriole

Icterus cucullatus

Size: 8" (20 cm)

Female: A dull yellow head, breast, belly, rump and tail. Gray wings and back. White wing bar. Black eyes.

Male: orange yellow with black throat, dark wings

Juvenile: similar to adult of the same sex

Nest: pendulous; female and male construct; 1–2 broods per year

Eggs: 3–5; dull white with brown markings

Incubation: 12–14 days; female incubates

Fledging: 12–14 days; female and male feed young

Migration: complete, to Central and South America

Food: insects, fruit, nectar

Compare: Female Bullock's Oriole (p. 433) is very similar, but has a pale white belly. Female Scott's Oriole (p. 437) is larger with black on the throat and upper breast.

Stan's Notes: A bird of tree-lined creeks and streams, palm groves, mesquite and arid scrub, often near suburbs. Male courts female with bows while hopping around her, singing a soft song. Points his bill skyward (like many birds in the blackbird family). Female will respond with a similar dance. Constructs an unusual sock-like nest, hung from a twig or woven through a palm leaf. Entrance often near the top, but can be on the side. Takes 3–7 days to build nest of wiry green grass, shredded palm leaves or yucca fibers. Some repair and reuse nests. Sips flower nectar, but not like hummingbirds. Often slices into the base of a flower, bypassing its natural entrance. Young are fed a regurgitate of insects and nectar the first 5–7 days of life.

male

female

Scott's Oriole
Icterus parisorum

Size: 9" (22.5 cm)

Male: Black head, neck, back, upper breast and tail. Lemon-yellow belly, shoulders and rump. Long, pointed, slightly down-curved black bill. Dark eyes. Two white wing bars.

Female: similar to male, but has much less black

Juvenile: grayer than female, yellow under belly only

Nest: pendulous; female builds; 1–2 broods a year

Eggs: 2–4; pale blue with brown markings

Incubation: 14–16 days; female and male incubate

Fledging: 14–16 days; female and male feed young

Migration: complete, to Mexico

Food: insects, fruit, nectar; will come to orange or grapefruit halves and nectar feeders

Compare: The female Bullock's Oriole (p. 433) has a pale-white belly. Male American Goldfinch (p. 423) is much smaller and has black on the forehead, not on the entire head.

Stan's Notes: Found in open dry areas often associated with yucca and palm. Like other oriole species, female constructs a sock-like pouch that hangs from the end of a thin branch or is woven into a hole in a palm leaf. Populations have increased over the past 100 years due to planting of palm trees. Male is yellow, not orange, like other male orioles. Hunts by gleaning insects and caterpillars from leaves. Uses its long, pointed bill to poke holes in bases of flowers to get nectar. Parents feed their young by regurgitating a mixture of insects and fruit. Named after General Winfield Scott, who fought in the Mexican War.

Western Kingbird
Tyrannus verticalis

Size: 9" (22.5 cm)

Male: Bright-yellow belly and yellow under wings. Gray head and chest, often with white chin. Wings and tail are dark gray to nearly black with white outer edges on tail.

Female: same as male

Juvenile: similar to adult, less yellow and more gray

Nest: cup; female and male construct; 1 brood per year

Eggs: 3–4; white with brown markings

Incubation: 18–20 days; female incubates

Fledging: 16–18 days; female and male feed young

Migration: complete, to Central America

Food: insects, berries

Compare: Western Meadowlark (p. 441) shares the yellow belly of Western Kingbird, but it has a distinctive black V-shaped necklace.

Stan's Notes: A bird of open country, frequently seen sitting on top of the same shrub or fence post. Hunts by watching for crickets, bees, grasshoppers and other insects and flying out to catch them, then returns to perch. Parents teach young how to hunt, bringing wounded insects back to the nest for the young to chase. Returns in March. Builds nest in April, often in a fork of a small single-trunk tree. Common in most of California, nesting in trees around farms or homesteads.

Western Meadowlark
Sturnella neglecta

YEAR-ROUND

Size:	9" (22.5 cm)
Male:	Heavy-bodied bird with a short tail. Yellow chest and brown back. Prominent V-shaped black necklace. White outer tail feathers.
Female:	same as male
Juvenile:	same as adult
Nest:	cup, on the ground in dense cover; female builds; 2 broods per year
Eggs:	3–5; white with brown markings
Incubation:	13–15 days; female incubates
Fledging:	11–13 days; female and male feed young
Migration:	non-migrator to partial migrator; moves around in winter to find food
Food:	insects, seeds
Compare:	Western Kingbird (p. 439) shares the yellow belly, but it lacks the V-shaped black necklace. The Horned Lark (p. 167) is smaller and has a white lower chest and belly. Look for a black V marking on the chest to help identify the Meadowlark.

Stan's Notes: Most common in open country. Named "Meadowlark" because it's a bird of meadows and sings like the larks of Europe. Not in the lark family; it's a member of the blackbird family. Best known for its wonderful song—a flute-like, clear whistle. Often seen perching on fence posts but quickly dives into tall grass when approached. Like other members of the blackbird family, the meadowlark catches prey by poking its long, thin bill in places such as holes in the ground or tufts of grass, where insects are hiding. Conspicuous white marks on sides of tail, seen when flying away.

BIRDING ON THE INTERNET

Birding online is a great way to discover additional information and learn more about birds. These websites will assist you in your pursuit of birds. Web addresses sometimes change a bit, so if one no longer works, just enter the name of the group into a search engine to track down the new address.

Site	Address
Author Stan Tekiela's homepage	naturesmart.com
American Birding Association	aba.org
Audubon California	ca.audubon.org
California Raptor Center	crc.vetmed.ucdavis.edu
The Cornell Lab of Ornithology	birds.cornell.edu
eBird	ebird.org
Golden Gate Audubon Society	goldengateaudubon.org
Hamilton Raptor Center	www.norcalraptors911.org
Ojai Raptor Center	www.ojairaptorcenter.org
San Fernando Valley Audubon Society	www.sfvaudubon.org

CHECKLIST/INDEX BY SPECIES

Use the boxes to check the birds you've seen.

MORE FOR CALIFORNIA BY STAN TEKIELA

Nature Books
Bald Eagles
Bird Trivia
Hummingbirds
Stan Tekiela's Birding for
    Beginners: California
Start Mushrooming
A Year in Nature with Stan Tekiela

Our Love of Wildlife Series
Our Love of Loons
Our Love of Owls

Wildlife Appreciation Series
Backyard Birds
Bears
Bird Migration
Cranes, Herons & Egrets
Deer, Elk & Moose
Intriguing Owls
Wild Birds

Nature Appreciation Series
Bird Nests
Feathers
Wildflowers

Nature's Wild Cards (playing cards)
Bears
Birds of the Northwest
Birds of the Southwest
Hummingbirds
Loons
Mammals of the Northwest
Mammals of the Southwest
Owls
Raptors
Trees of the Northwest
Trees of the Southwest

ABOUT THE AUTHOR

Naturalist, wildlife photographer and writer **Stan Tekiela** is the originator of the popular state-specific field guide series that includes the *Birds of Arizona Field Guide*. Stan has authored more than 190 educational books, including field guides, quick guides, nature books, children's books, and more, presenting many species of animals and plants.

With a Bachelor of Science degree in natural history from the University of Minnesota and as an active professional naturalist for more than 30 years, Stan studies and photographs wildlife throughout the United States and Canada. He has received national and regional awards for his books and photographs and is also a well-known columnist and radio personality. His syndicated column appears in more than 25 newspapers, and his wildlife programs are broadcast on a number of Midwest radio stations. You can follow Stan on Facebook and Twitter or contact him via his website, naturesmart.com.